# CLEAVING to CLIMAX

## PRACTICAL STEPS FOR DEEPENING MARITAL BONDS

**BERTHA BERNASKO ASANTE**

Copyright Bertha Bernasko Asante @ 2024 Breakfree Forever Publishing

ALL RIGHTS RESERVED. No part of this book may be reproduced or transmitted in any form whatsoever, electronic or mechanical, including photocopying and recording any informational storage or retrieval system, without the express written, dated and signed with permission from the author. Author: Bertha Bernasko Asante

**Title:** Cleaving to Climax ISBN: 978-1-0686737-2-6

**Category:** Human Spiritual /Marriage / Relationships

LIMITS OF LIABILITY/DISCLAIMER OF WARRANTY: The author and publisher of this book have used their best efforts in preparing this material. The author and publisher make no representation or warranties with respect to the accuracy, applicability or completeness of the contents. They disclaim any warranties (expressed or implied), or merchantability for any particular purpose. The author and publisher shall in no event be held liable for any loss or other damages, including (but not limited to) special, incidental, consequential or other damages. The information presented in this publication is compiled from sources believed to be accurate. However, the publisher assumes no responsibility for errors or omissions. The information in this publication is not intended to replace or substitute professional advice. The author and publisher specifically disclaim any liability, loss, or risk that is incurred as a consequence, directly or indirectly, of the use and application of any of the contents of this work. Printed in the United Kingdom.

# DEDICATION

I dedicate this book to my respectable cherished parents, Mr and Mrs Abban, who have led by example and inspired me to become the person I am today.

To my dear husband, Samuel who has supported me and allowed me to flourish as a wife, motivating me daily to strive for excellence. To my three precious children, and my children in Christ, who have touched my heart with their dedication and commitment to take on board every godly counsel I throw at them.

To all couples navigating the beautiful journey of marriage, may this book be a guiding light, helping you discover the profound depths of intimacy and connection.

This book is dedicated to all of you, with boundless love and gratitude.

# FOREWORD

It is with deep joy and heartfelt pride that we pen this foreword for "Cleaving to Climax: Practical Steps for Deepening Marital Bonds," a work that beautifully captures the essence of marital intimacy and reflects the wisdom and experience of its author, Deaconess Mrs. Bertha Bernasko Asante.

Bertha's journey towards becoming a respected marriage counsellor and author has been one of intentional growth, shaped by both her personal experiences and the exemplary marriages she has been privileged to witness. Raised in a family where love, faith, and commitment were the foundation stones, Bertha grew up observing the enduring bond between her parents. Now in their eighties, they remain a living testament to the power of intimate, God-centred love—a love that has weathered the years and continues to inspire those around them.

Bertha's own marriage to Samuel has been another beacon of hope and example of what it means to build and sustain a relationship based on mutual respect, intentional effort, and unwavering faith. Together, they have not only built a home but a partnership that exemplifies the principles she shares in this book. Their union reflects the ideals Bertha advocates for—one that is intentionally nurtured, filled with love, and rooted in the shared goal of growing together in Christ.

We have had the privilege of mentoring Bertha in our home, as Eva's little sister, where she served as our maid of honour and where her passion for strong, healthy marriages was first evident. Over the years, she has grown into a trusted voice in our church community, regularly ministering to our congregation at Believers Bible Christian Church and offering marriage counselling to our members. The warmth and respect with which she is received are testaments to her sincerity, wisdom, and the deep connection she fosters with those she serves.

"Cleaving to Climax..." is not just a book; it is a heartfelt guide crafted from years of personal experience, spiritual insight, and counselling. It is a reflection of Bertha's life journey—a journey marked by her upbringing, her own thriving marriage, and her commitment to helping others achieve the same depth of intimacy in their relationships.

As you delve into the pages of this book, we trust you will find inspiration, practical advice, and spiritual guidance that will help you and your spouse build a stronger, more intimate bond. Bertha's unique blend of biblical wisdom and practical insights offers a roadmap for anyone seeking to enhance their marital relationship.

We are honoured to have witnessed Bertha's growth and to have played a part in her spiritual journey. We know that this book will be a blessing to many, just as she has been a blessing to us and our community.

**Bishop Peter Hemeng**
**Rev. Mrs. Eva-Vera Hemeng**
*Believers Bible Christian Church*

Deaconess Bertha Asante has always been more than a mentor to those she oversees—she has been a spiritual mother, family guide, and trusted confidant. Her wisdom and practical advice on marriage, which she generously shares on my YouTube channel, podcast, and TikTok, have deeply impacted many lives.

Affectionately called "Mummy Bertha," she is not only rich in knowledge but lives out what she teaches. I've always admired how she and her husband, Deacon Sam Asante, open their home with warmth and love, offering mentorship and support to couples. Though Bertha is the author of this powerful book, the life she and her husband share provides a shining example of the principles within.

It's incredibly exciting to see her insights captured in this book. Her counsel has blessed so many, and now, through these pages, countless others will benefit from her wisdom and life-changing guidance.

**Foreword by**

**Evelyn Kyei**
*Grace for Living*

# CONTENTS

| | | |
|---|---|---|
| **DEDICATION** | | 3 |
| **INTRODUCTION** | | 8 |
| Chapter 1: | Leaving: A Prerequisite for Cleaving | 11 |
| Chapter 2: | Cleaving: An Assurance After Leaving | 19 |
| Chapter 3: | Exploring The Various Dimensions | 27 |
| Chapter 4: | Can a Marriage Survive Without Intimacy? | 55 |
| Chapter 5: | Long-Distant Couples | 67 |
| Chapter 6: | Common Marital Mistakes | 71 |
| Chapter 7: | Practical Tips and Biblical Insights | 81 |
| Chapter 8: | The Living Word on Cleaving and Intimacy | 85 |
| Chapter 9: | Biblical Principles on Sexuality | 99 |
| Chapter 10: | Christian Views on Sex | 103 |
| Chapter 11: | Sexual Enhancement for Couples | 109 |
| Chapter 12: | 20 Love Language for Couples | 121 |
| Chapter 13: | The Benefits of Cordial Intimacy | 125 |
| **FINAL COUNSEL** | | 128 |
| **CONCLUSION** | | 129 |
| **ACKNOWLEDGMENTS** | | 130 |
| **AUTHOR BIOGRAPHY** | | 132 |

# INTRODUCTION

This precious book delves into the profound and multifaceted concept of intimacy in relationships. Cleaving, often considered the heart of a deep and meaningful connection between couples, goes beyond physical closeness. It encompasses emotional, intellectual, and spiritual bonds that unite people, allowing them to share their most authentic selves.

At the core of intimacy lies the idea of "cleaving," a term that signifies a deep, abiding union between partners. Cleaving is more than just a physical connection; it is an intertwining of lives, aspirations, and emotions. It represents a commitment to navigate the complexities of life together, to support and uplift each other, and to grow both individually and as a unit.

The phrase "to leave and to cleave" comes from the Bible, specifically in Genesis 2:24 (KJV), which states, "Therefore shall a man leave his father and his mother and shall cleave unto his wife: and they shall be one flesh." This passage lays a foundational principle for marriage in Christian teachings. Let us explore its meaning and implications for sex and intimacy in marriage:

The biblical principle of "to leave and to cleave" provides a framework for understanding the deep, multifaceted bond that marriage entails. It emphasises prioritising the marital relationship, fostering emotional and physical intimacy, supporting, and depending on each other, communicating openly, and maintaining a lifelong commitment. These elements are essential for a healthy, fulfilling sexual relationship and overall intimacy in marriage. By adhering to this principle, couples can build a strong, intimate, and enduring marital relationship.

This book aims to provide readers like you with insights into achieving and maintaining a high level of intimacy in your relationships. It offers practical advice, real-life examples, and exercises designed to help partners deepen their connection on all levels. Through understanding and embracing the concept of cleaving, you can experience the true climax of intimacy—a profound, enduring bond that enriches your live and sustains your relationship through all of life's challenges and triumphs.

By exploring the principles of cleaving, you will discover the transformative power of genuine intimacy. You will learn how to communicate more effectively, nurture mutual respect, and cultivate a loving and supportive environment.

Take note that intimacy will be used interchangeably with cleaving along the line, depending on the subject matter.

The scenarios presented are based on real-life situations managed with my clients, with names changed for confidentiality's sake. This narrative of real-life circumstances about intimacy in relationships seeks to empower couples to build connections that are not only resilient and enduring but also deeply satisfying and joyously intimate.

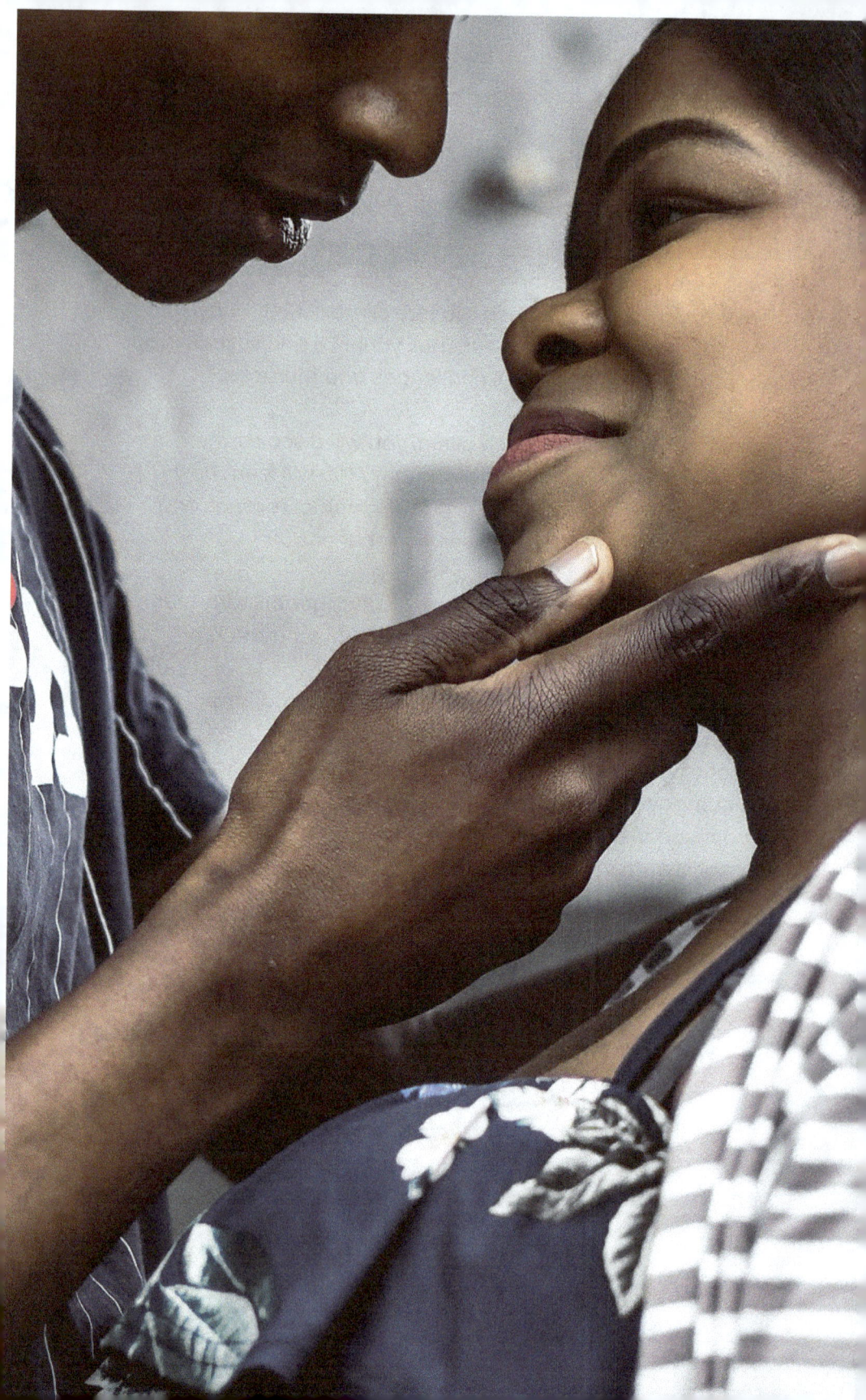

**CHAPTER 1**

# LEAVING A PREREQUISITE FOR CLEAVING

# CH 1: Leaving - A Prerequisite of Cleaving

In the journey of transforming, one's life and relationship, the concept of leaving serves as a crucial prerequisite for the process of cleaving. To cleave is to bind closely and steadfastly, to form deep connections and commitments. However, before one can fully embrace the act of cleaving, they must first be willing to let go of the past, detach from old patterns, beliefs, and relationships that no longer serve them. Leaving represents a necessary shedding of the old to make space for the new, a process of releasing attachments and stepping into the unknown with courage and openness. By acknowledging the importance of leaving behind what no longer aligns with their true selves, individuals can create the necessary space and clarity to cleave authentically and wholeheartedly to what truly matters in their lives.

> Leaving behind the familiar creates space for a deeper union where true partnership can thrive.
> ~ Bertha Bernasko Asante

## The components of leaving before cleaving

In the quest for deep and meaningful relationships, the components of leaving before cleaving are paramount. Central to this process are the crucial steps of separating from one's parental influences and cultivating independence within the context of the marital union. Navigating these components is often intricate and demanding, as the deep-rooted connections to one's family of origin can impede the formation of a new, self-sufficient household. This scenario highlights the common challenges couples face in disentangling themselves from parental dependencies and the journey towards establishing autonomy within their relationship. Through insightful best practices and guided transformation, we delve into how couples can successfully navigate these complexities and forge a harmonious path towards a truly intimate and fulfilling union.

### Separation from parents

Separation from parents in the context of marriage involves the essential process of prioritising one's spouse and the marital relationship above familial ties. It signifies a shift in loyalty and responsibilities, where the focus is on building a strong partnership and shared life with one's significant other. This separation does not imply cutting off family relationships but rather establishing healthy boundaries that uphold the sanctity of the marital union. By navigating this transition thoughtfully and respectfully, couples can lay the foundation for a harmonious and fulfilling marriage built on mutual respect, support, and unity.

### Independence

Independence in marriage underscores the importance of establishing a new, autonomous household where the couple makes decisions collaboratively, free from undue parental influence. This independence allows couples to develop their own values, routines, and problem-solving strategies, tailored to their unique relationship dynamics. It encourages mutual respect and shared responsibility, fostering a sense of partnership and unity. By prioritising their collective decision-making, couples can create a supportive and empowering environment, essential for nurturing a healthy, balanced, and fulfilling marital life. This independence is crucial for the couple's growth, resilience, and long-term success.

## The practicalities of leaving

Let us analyse this scenario about a couple regarding their challenges with separation from parents and independence in marriage.

**My clients,** John and Emily, have been married for three years. Unresolved issues with their families of origin have strained their relationship, despite their love for each other. John's parents are particularly involved in their lives, often offering unsolicited advice, and expecting frequent visits. Emily, while initially welcoming of John's family, has grown frustrated by the constant interference and John's inability to set boundaries.

John's mother, Mrs. Thompson, frequently calls to check on them, offer advice on household matters, and even drop by unannounced. She often critiques Emily's cooking, housekeeping, and even their decisions regarding their child. John, not wanting to upset his mother, seldom intervenes, leaving Emily feeling unsupported and disrespected.

The situation reached a boiling point when Mrs. Thompson insisted on organising their child's first birthday party, disregarding Emily's plans. Emily felt sidelined and invalidated, leading to a major argument between her and John. She expressed her feelings of being secondary in John's life, which he initially dismissed, claiming she was overreacting.

**My recommended Best Practice of Implementation to John and Emily included:**

**Intervention and Guidance:** Recognising the detrimental impact of this dynamic on their marriage, John and Emily sought counselling. During the sessions, they learnt the importance of prioritising their marriage and establishing independence from their parents. I emphasised two key areas for improvement:

**Separation from Parents:** Understanding the Shift in Loyalty: John needed to understand that his primary loyalty and responsibility should be towards Emily. This did not mean abandoning his parents but rather reprioritising his commitments.

**Setting Boundaries:** They were guided to set clear boundaries with their parents, particularly John with his mother. John was encouraged to have a heartfelt conversation with his parents, explaining the need for space and respect for their decisions as a couple.

**Establishing Independence:**

**Decision-Making as a Couple:** John and Emily were taught to make decisions together without external influence. This included managing their household, planning events, and parenting their child.

**Building a United Front:** They practiced presenting a united front to their families, ensuring that any decisions communicated to their parents were jointly made and agreed upon.

**Implementation:** John had a difficult but necessary conversation with his mother, explaining the importance of giving him and Emily space to grow as a couple. He assured her of his love but emphasised the need to respect their autonomy. John and Emily also established a weekly couple's meeting to discuss any family-related issues and decide on their responses together.

### Fruitful Outcome:

Over time, the changes began to yield positive results. Mrs. Thompson, while initially hurt, gradually adapted to the new boundaries. She started to respect John and Emily's decisions and reduced her unsolicited involvement. Emily felt more valued and respected, leading to a significant improvement in their marital satisfaction.

John and Emily's relationship flourished as they embraced their independence. They found joy in making joint decisions and handling household matters together. Their home became a haven of mutual respect and love, free from external pressures. The couple's newfound ability to manage their relationship dynamics strengthened their bond, paving the way for a deeper and more intimate connection.

Through prioritising their marriage and establishing a new, independent household, John and Emily experienced the profound benefits of cleaving. Their relationship became a model of mutual respect and partnership, demonstrating the transformative power of appropriate separation from parents and the establishment of marital independence.

### Wisdom Nuggets for Leaving

**Prioritise Partnership:** The foundation of a strong marriage begins with the ability to prioritise your partner above all others, including family. This shift allows couples to build their own unique bond and establish a life together.

**Embrace Independence:** Leaving is not just a physical act but an emotional and psychological shift towards independence, allowing each partner to make decisions and grow together as a unified front.

**Healthy boundaries foster growth:** Establishing boundaries with extended family is crucial for the growth of a new marriage. These boundaries create space for the couple to develop their own identity and traditions.

 **Leaving requires letting go:** To truly leave, one must let go of past dependencies and expectations, creating a clean slate for the marriage to flourish without the shadow of past influences.

 **Courage to Transition:** Leaving requires courage and a willingness to step into the unknown with your partner, trusting that this transition will lead to deeper connection and mutual support.

> In stepping away from the past, couples build a foundation for a future where their unity becomes the cornerstone.
> ~ *Bertha Bernasko Asante*

# CHAPTER 2
# CLEAVING AN ASSURANCE AFTER LEAVING

> Cleaving is the art of building a bond that withstands the tests of time, rooted in trust and unwavering commitment.
>
> ~ Bertha Bernasko Asante

## The components of cleaving after leaving

In marriage, the concept of "cleaving after leaving" emphasises the importance of forming a strong bond and attachment with one's spouse after establishing independence from parental influences. This process involves prioritising the marital relationship and creating a new, shared life together. However, many couples struggle with maintaining this bond, often due to a lack of unity. When couples fail to fully commit to one another, their relationship may lack the deep emotional and spiritual connection necessary for true unity. Without this foundation, misunderstandings and conflicts can arise, leading to feelings of isolation and dissatisfaction. By focussing on bonding and attachment, couples can cultivate a resilient partnership, fostering a sense of unity that enhances their overall relationship. This journey requires continuous effort, open communication, and mutual respect, creating a harmonious and fulfilling marital life.

## Bonding and Attachment

To cleave in marriage means to adhere firmly and closely to one's spouse, symbolising a strong and enduring bond. This bonding and attachment go beyond mere physical presence; it involves deep emotional, psychological, and sometimes spiritual connections. Couples who cleave to each other cultivate a partnership built on mutual trust, respect, and unwavering support. This enduring bond becomes the foundation of their relationship, enabling them to weather challenges together. By prioritising their connection, couples create a secure and nurturing environment where love can flourish, fostering a sense of belonging and unity that strengthens their marriage over time.

## Unity and Oneness

Unity and oneness in marriage refer to a profound, intimate union that encompasses physical, emotional, and spiritual dimensions. When a couple becomes "one flesh," it signifies more than just physical intimacy; it reflects a deep emotional and spiritual synchronisation where their lives are intricately intertwined. This holistic connection means that partners understand and support each other's innermost desires, fears, and aspirations. They share a common purpose and values, enhancing their sense of togetherness. Achieving this level of unity and oneness requires continuous effort, communication, and empathy, creating a harmonious and resilient relationship where both individuals feel deeply connected and understood.

Cleaving in a marriage entails creating a strong and enduring bond, where spouses adhere firmly and closely to each other. This bond is essential for achieving unity and oneness, encompassing physical, emotional, and spiritual connections. The following scenario illustrates the common missteps couples might make in this area and the successful strategies they implemented to enhance their marital bond.

## The Practicalities of Cleaving

Let us examine the situation of a couple client and their challenges with bonding, attachment, unity, and oneness:

My clients, Michael and Sarah, have been married for five years. Despite their initial strong connection, their relationship has become strained due to their inability to truly bond and achieve unity. They both have demanding careers and, over time, have drifted into parallel lives rather than a shared journey.

### Wrong Practices in Bonding and Attachment:

**Lack of Quality Time:** Michael and Sarah often prioritise their careers and personal interests over spending quality time together. They rarely engage in meaningful conversations, opting instead to discuss daily routines.

**Neglecting Emotional Support:** When Sarah feels stressed or upset, Michael often dismisses her feelings, suggesting she "toughen up" rather than offering empathy and support. Similarly, Sarah tends to ignore Michael's need for emotional reassurance, focussing more on her own challenges.

**Separate Pursuits:** They spend their free time on individual hobbies and activities, seldom finding common interests to enjoy together. This separation leads to a lack of shared experiences and memories.

## Wrong Practice in Unity and Oneness:

**Physical Distance:** Michael and Sarah's physical intimacy has diminished, with both feeling disconnected and unfulfilled. They rarely engage in affectionate gestures like holding hands or hugging.

**Emotional Disconnection:** They avoid discussing deeper feelings and thoughts, fearing conflict or discomfort. This results in an emotional gap where they are unaware of each other's inner worlds.

**Spiritual Disconnection:** They avoid discussing deeper feelings and thoughts, fearing conflict or discomfort. This results in an emotional gap where they are unaware of each other's inner worlds.

## Best Practice Implementation

### Intervention and Guidance

Realising the detrimental effects of their habits on their marriage, Michael and Sarah sought counselling. During the counselling sessions, they learnt the significance of bonding and attachment, as well as achieving unity and oneness. I offered them practical steps to improve their relationship, which included:

## Bonding and Attachment:

**Prioritising Quality Time:** Michael and Sarah's physical intimacy has diminished, with both feeling disconnected and unfulfilled. They rarely engage in affectionate gestures like holding hands or hugging.

**Emotional Support and Empathy:** They learnt to validate each other's emotions and offer genuine support. Michael practiced active listening, while Sarah focused on being more empathetic to Michael's needs.

**Shared Interests and Activities:** The couple was advised to find common hobbies and interests to enjoy together, creating opportunities for shared experiences and bonding.

### Unity and Oneness:

**Enhancing Physical Intimacy:** Michael and Sarah were guided to rekindle their physical connection through small, consistent gestures of affection and regular intimate time together.

**Deepening Emotional Connection:** They committed to open and honest communication about their feelings, dreams, and fears. This involved setting aside time for deeper conversations and being vulnerable with each other.

**Spiritual Growth Together:** They explored their spiritual beliefs as a couple, attending the same place of worship and engaging in discussions about their spiritual journeys. This included praying together and participating in spiritual activities that reinforced their shared values.

### Implementation

Michael and Sarah began by scheduling weekly date nights, ensuring that these times were sacred and free from work or other distractions. They also established a daily routine of sharing their "highs and lows" of the day, fostering open communication and emotional support.

To reignite their physical connection, they tried to engage in affectionate gestures like holding hands, hugging, and spending intimate time together regularly. They also explored new hobbies together, such as hiking and cooking, which helped them create new shared memories.

For their spiritual growth, Michael and Sarah started attending the same place of worship and discussed their experiences and reflections afterward. They also began a nightly practice of praying together, which brought a new level of spiritual intimacy to their relationship.

### Fruitful Outcome
Over time, these changes brought significant positive outcomes. Michael and Sarah felt more connected and supported in their marriage. Their emotional intimacy deepened as they shared their inner worlds and offered mutual support. The physical affection they reintroduced into their relationship rekindled their passion and sense of closeness.

Spiritually, they found a new level of unity, sharing their beliefs and values in a way that strengthened their bond. The combination of these practices led to a profound sense of oneness, where Michael and Sarah viewed their marriage as a united front, tackling life's challenges together.

Through the intentional practice of bonding and attachment, and striving for unity and oneness, Michael and Sarah transformed their relationship into a deeply intimate and fulfilling partnership. Their journey illustrates the power of cleaving in marriage, creating a resilient and joyful union that thrives on shared love and connection.

### Wisdom Nuggets for Cleaving
**Strength in Unity:**
- True cleaving involves a deep, abiding bond where partners hold fast to each other, creating strength and resilience through unity and shared purpose.

**Emotional vulnerability builds trust:**
- Cleaving thrives on emotional vulnerability, where openness and honesty cultivate trust and understanding, essential elements of a lasting relationship.

**Mutual support is key:**
- In cleaving, each partner offers unwavering support and encouragement, recognising that their individual strengths contribute to the success of the marriage.

**Intimacy Deepens Connection:**
- Intimacy in cleaving goes beyond the physical, encompassing emotional, spiritual, and intellectual bonds that deepen the connection between partners.

**Commitment Through Change:**
- Cleaving is about steadfast commitment through life's changes and challenges, providing assurance and stability to weather any storm together.

*In the journey of marriage, cleaving assures us that together we are stronger, more resilient, and more fulfilled.*

*~ Bertha Bernasko Asante*

# CHAPTER 3
# EXPLORING THE VARIOUS DIMENSIONS OF INTIMACY IN CLEAVING

**Cleaving and intimacy in marriage encompasses a deep emotional, spiritual, and physical connection between spouses. It goes beyond** mere physical affection to include trust, vulnerability, and a sense of unity.

*The deepest connections are forged in vulnerability, where trust and empathy create an unbreakable bond.*

*~ Bertha Bernasko Asante*

Intimacy in marriage is nurtured through communication, mutual respect, and a commitment to prioritise the relationship. It requires effort from both spouses to maintain and deepen over time, contributing to a strong and fulfilling marital bond. Here are some key aspects of intimacy in marriage:

**Emotional intimacy:** This involves sharing feelings, thoughts, and experiences openly with your spouse. It is about being able to empathise with each other's emotions, supporting each other through challenges, and celebrating joys together.

**Spiritual Intimacy:** For couples who share a faith, spiritual intimacy involves praying together, discussing spiritual matters, and growing in faith as a couple. It deepens the bond by aligning spiritual values and beliefs.

**Physical Intimacy:** This includes sexual expression within marriage but also extends to non-sexual physical affection such as holding hands, hugging, kissing, and cuddling. Physical intimacy fosters closeness and affection between spouses.

**Intellectual Intimacy:** Engaging in meaningful conversations, sharing intellectual interests, and respecting each other's thoughts and opinions are aspects of intellectual intimacy. It involves stimulating each other intellectually and growing together mentally.

**Recreational intimacy:** Sharing leisure activities and hobbies can strengthen marital intimacy by creating shared experiences and fostering enjoyment together.

**Relational intimacy:** building a strong friendship forms the basis of relational intimacy. It involves being best friends, supporting each other's personal growth, and enjoying each other's company.

By addressing and enhancing emotional, intellectual, spiritual, and physical intimacy, couples can achieve a deeper and more fulfilling connection of cleaving. These situations illustrate the transformative power of intentional practices in building intimacy, leading to resilient and joyful relationships.

> Sharing feelings among couples strengthens connections.
>
> ~ Bertha Bernasko Asante

## Emotional Intimacy

Emotional intimacy involves sharing feelings, thoughts, and experiences at a deep level. Emotional intimacy creates a safe space for partners to express their vulnerabilities, fears, and dreams without judgment. It fosters trust and empathy, which are essential for a resilient relationship.

Emotional intimacy is a cornerstone of a healthy and fulfilling relationship. It involves the ability to share one's deepest sensations, judgement, and capabilities with a partner in a manner that is open, honest, and free of judgement. This level of sharing creates a safe space where both partners feel valued and understood, paving the way for a deeper connection.

At its core, emotional intimacy is about vulnerability. It requires each partner to reveal their innermost fears, dreams, and insecurities, trusting that they will be met with empathy and support rather than criticism or dismissal. This vulnerability fosters a sense of trust, which is crucial for the relationship to endure challenges and grow stronger over time.

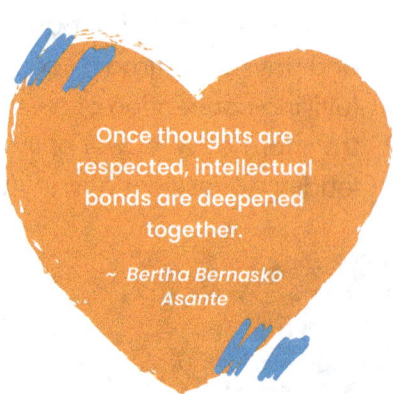

Once thoughts are respected, intellectual bonds are deepened together.

~ Bertha Bernasko Asante

Furthermore, emotional intimacy promotes empathy. When partners can see the world through each other's eyes, they develop a deeper understanding and appreciation for one another. This empathy creates a foundation of compassion and support that strengthens the relationship.

## Practicalities of Emotional Intimacy

Let us analyse the situation of a couple regarding their quest to build emotional intimacy.

My clients, David and Laura, have been married for ten years. Over time, they realised that they had started to drift apart emotionally. Their conversations had become superficial, revolving mostly around work and household chores rather than their feelings and aspirations.

### Wrong Practice

David and Laura would come home from work and focus on their own activities—David would watch TV, and Laura would browse social media. They rarely talked about their feelings or shared personal experiences from their day. When conflicts arose, they often avoided discussing them, leading to unresolved issues and growing emotional distance.

My Recommended Best Practice for Implementation:

### Guidance:

**Scheduled Quality Time:** They were advised to set aside dedicated time each day to talk without distractions, focussing on their feelings and thoughts.

**Active Listening and Empathy:** They practiced active listening, ensuring that when one spoke, the other listened attentively without interrupting. They also learnt to empathise with each other's experiences.

**Sharing Vulnerabilities:** They were encouraged to share their fears, dreams, and vulnerabilities openly, creating a safe space for emotional expression.

## Practicalities of Emotional Intimacy

Let us analyse the situation of a couple regarding their quest to build emotional intimacy.

My clients, David and Laura, have been married for ten years. Over time, they realised that they had started to drift apart emotionally. Their conversations had become superficial, revolving mostly around work and household chores rather than their feelings and aspirations.

## Wrong Practice

David and Laura would come home from work and focus on their own activities—David would watch TV, and Laura would browse social media. They rarely talked about their feelings or shared personal experiences from their day. When conflicts arose, they often avoided discussing them, leading to unresolved issues and growing emotional distance.

My Recommended Best Practice for Implementation:

## Guidance:

**Scheduled Quality Time:** They were advised to set aside dedicated time each day to talk without distractions, focussing on their feelings and thoughts.

**Active Listening and Empathy:** They practiced active listening, ensuring that when one spoke, the other listened attentively without interrupting. They also learnt to empathise with each other's experiences.

**Sharing Vulnerabilities:** They were encouraged to share their fears, dreams, and vulnerabilities openly, creating a safe space for emotional expression.

**Implementation:**
David and Laura started a nightly ritual where they spent 30 minutes together without any distractions, talking about their day, feelings, and anything on their minds. They practiced active listening and validated each other's feelings. They also began to address conflicts calmly and constructively, ensuring that both felt heard and understood.

**Fruitful Outcome:**
Over time, David and Laura's emotional intimacy deepened significantly. They felt more connected and understood, and their relationship became more resilient to challenges. The trust and empathy they developed fostered a stronger emotional bond, making their marriage more fulfilling.

Vulnerability is the bridge to insight among couples.

~ Bertha Bernasko Asante

## Wisdom Nuggets for Emotional Intimacy

 **The Heart of Understanding:** Emotional intimacy thrives on empathy and active listening, allowing partners to feel truly heard and understood. This forms the foundation of trust and compassion in a relationship.

 **Share Your Inner World:** Openly sharing your inner thoughts and emotions creates a safe space for vulnerability, strengthening the emotional connection between partners.

 **Celebrate and Comfort Together:** Celebrating joys and supporting each other during challenges enhances emotional closeness, reinforcing that you are a team through life's ups and downs.

 **Emotional presence is key:** Being emotionally present and attentive to your partner's needs fosters a deeper bond and ensures that both partners feel valued and cherished.

 **Cultivate emotional resilience:** Building emotional resilience together helps couples navigate conflicts and misunderstandings, turning challenges into opportunities for growth.

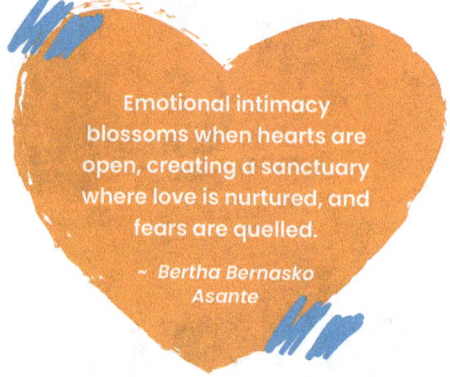

Emotional intimacy blossoms when hearts are open, creating a sanctuary where love is nurtured, and fears are quelled.

~ Bertha Bernasko Asante

## Intellectual Intimacy

Intellectual intimacy arises from the sharing of principles, values, beliefs, and philosophies. It involves stimulating conversations, mutual respect for each other's viewpoints, and a continuous exchange of knowledge. This type of intimacy nurtures a mental connection that keeps the relationship intellectually engaging and fulfilling.

Intellectual intimacy is a crucial aspect of a thriving relationship, characterised by the sharing and exploration of suggestions, ideas, and convictions between partners. This form of intimacy fosters a mental connection that keeps the relationship intellectually stimulating and deeply engaging.

At the heart of intellectual intimacy is the willingness to engage in meaningful and thought-provoking conversations. These discussions allow partners to explore each other's perspectives and challenge each other's thinking, leading to personal growth and a deeper understanding of one another. Engaging in such dialogues can range from discussing current events and philosophical questions to sharing personal dreams and goals.

each other's viewpoints, and a continuous exchange of knowledge. This type of intimacy nurtures a mental connection that keeps the relationship intellectually engaging and fulfilling.

Intellectual intimacy is a crucial aspect of a thriving relationship, characterised by the sharing and exploration of suggestions, ideas, and convictions between partners. This form of intimacy fosters a mental connection that keeps the relationship intellectually stimulating and deeply engaging.

At the heart of intellectual intimacy is the willingness to engage in meaningful and thought-provoking conversations. These discussions allow partners to explore each other's perspectives and challenge each other's thinking, leading to personal growth and a deeper understanding of one another. Engaging in such dialogues can range from discussing current events and philosophical questions to sharing personal dreams and goals.

Intellectual intimacy nurtures a dynamic and fulfilling partnership. By maintaining an intellectually engaging relationship, couples can enjoy a vibrant connection that deepens their bond and contributes to a shared sense of purpose and growth.

> When couples' hearts connect, they reveal love's true strength.
>
> ~ Bertha Bernasko Asante

## Practicalities of Intellectual Intimacy

Let us explore the situation of a couple concerning their quest for building intellectual intimacy.

**My clients,** Mark and Jane, have been together for six years. They both have a strong intellectual curiosity but found that they seldom engaged in stimulating conversations with each other.

### Wrong Practice

Mark and Jane often spent their evenings engaged in separate activities—Mark reading in his study and Jane watching documentaries alone. They rarely discussed their thoughts, ideas, or the interesting things they learnt, leading to a lack of intellectual connection.

### My Recommended Best Practice for Implementation:

### Guidance:

**Shared Intellectual Activities:** They were encouraged to engage in intellectual activities together, such as reading the same book, watching documentaries, or attending lectures and discussing them.

> When couples explore the landscape of thought together, they forge a mental connection that is both engaging and enriching.
>
> ~ Bertha Bernasko Asante

**Stimulating Conversations:** They practiced having regular discussions about ideas, values, and beliefs, ensuring mutual respect for each other's viewpoints.

**Continuous Exchange of Knowledge:** They were advised to share new things they learnt with each other regularly.

### Implementation:

Mark and Jane chose a book to read together each month, setting aside time to discuss each chapter. They also scheduled weekly "intellectual dates" where they watched a documentary or attended a lecture and then discussed it in depth. They made a habit of sharing intriguing articles or facts they came across.

### Fruitful Outcome:

These practices nurtured a strong mental connection between Mark and Jane. Their relationship became more intellectually engaging and fulfilling, as they enjoyed stimulating conversations and learnt from each other. This intellectual intimacy added a new dimension to their bond, enhancing their overall connection.

> Intellectual intimacy is the meeting of minds, where shared ideas and stimulating conversations deepen understanding.
>
> ~ *Bertha Bernasko Asante*

## Wisdom Nuggets for Emotional Intimacy

 **Stimulate Each Other's Minds:** Intellectual intimacy involves engaging in thought-provoking conversations that challenge and inspire both partners, fostering mental growth.

 **Respect Diverse Perspectives:** Valuing and respecting each other's thoughts and opinions creates a rich tapestry of ideas, strengthening your intellectual bond.

 **Grow Together Mentally:** Sharing intellectual interests and pursuing knowledge together encourages personal growth and deepens your connection.

 **Embrace Curiosity:** Embracing curiosity and exploring new ideas as a couple keeps your relationship vibrant and intellectually stimulating.

 **Intellectual compatibility matters:** Cultivating intellectual compatibility ensures that you remain mentally engaged and connected throughout your relationship.

*As conversations spark, minds grow closer.*

~ Bertha Bernasko Asante

## Spiritual Intimacy

Spiritual intimacy is a profound aspect of a relationship that goes beyond physical and emotional connections, offering a deep sense of purpose and meaning. It involves the alignment of values and beliefs and a shared connection to something greater than oneself, whether that be faith, a spiritual path, or a shared philosophy about life.

As it transcends the fleshly and touching aspects of a relationship, it involves a united sense of standards, tenacity, principles, and a connection to something greater than oneself. This dimension of intimacy can provide profound meaning and direction to the relationship, enriching it with a sense of unity and shared destiny.

At its core, spiritual intimacy is about exploring the deeper questions of life together, such as the meaning of existence, the nature of the universe, and the couple's place within it. This exploration fosters a shared sense of purpose and direction, uniting partners in a journey that transcends everyday life. Engaging in spiritual practices together, such as meditation, prayer, or attending religious services, can strengthen this bond and provide a sense of peace and harmony in the relationship.

Spiritual intimacy also involves supporting each other's spiritual growth and respecting each other's beliefs. This mutual support creates an environment where both partners feel free to express their spiritual selves without fear of judgement or rejection.

By nurturing spiritual intimacy, couples can experience a sense of unity and shared destiny that enriches their relationship. This dimension of intimacy provides a solid foundation for weathering life's challenges and celebrating its joys, as it reinforces the bond between partners with a shared vision and commitment to each other's spiritual well-being. This profound connection can offer couples a deeper appreciation for each other and the

# CH 3: Exploring Imensions Of Intimacy In Cleaving

world around them, enhancing their partnership with lasting significance and fulfilment.

## Practicalities of Intellectual Intimacy

Let us evaluate the situation of another couple regarding their mission to build spiritual intimacy.

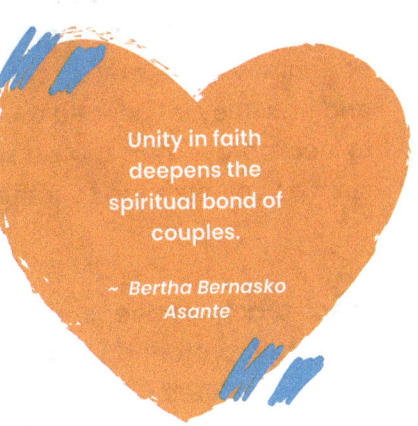

*Unity in faith deepens the spiritual bond of couples.*

~ Bertha Bernasko Asante

**My clients,** Alex and Mia, have been married for three years. Although they both value spirituality, they realised they were not sharing this important aspect of their lives with each other.

## Wrong Practice

Alex and Mia attended separate places of worship and rarely discussed their spiritual beliefs or experiences. They prayed and meditated separately, missing the opportunity to connect spiritually as a couple.

## My Recommended Best Practice for Implementation:

### Guidance:

**Shared Spiritual Activities:** They were encouraged to participate in spiritual practices together, such as attending the same place of worship, praying, or meditating together.

**Discussing Spiritual Beliefs:** They were advised to have regular discussions about their spiritual beliefs, values, and experiences.

**Shared Sense of Purpose:** They explored ways to align their life goals and values with their spiritual beliefs, creating a shared sense of purpose.

**CH 3:** Exploring Imensions Of Intimacy In Cleaving    *Cleaving To Climax*

### Implementation:
Alex and Mia started attending the same place of worship and set aside time each day to pray and meditate together. They also began having weekly discussions about their spiritual experiences and how they influenced their values and goals. They found ways to incorporate their shared spiritual beliefs into their daily lives, such as volunteering together.

### Fruitful Outcome:
These practices deepened Alex and Mia's spiritual intimacy, creating a profound sense of unity and shared destiny. They felt more connected on a deeper level, and their shared spiritual journey enriched their relationship with a sense of purpose and meaning.

> Shared beliefs create unbreakable spiritual connections.
>
> ~ Bertha Bernasko Asante

**CH 3:** Exploring Imensions Of Intimacy In Cleaving

## Wisdom Nuggets for Emotional Intimacy

**Shared Spiritual Journey:** Spiritual intimacy involves embarking on a shared spiritual journey, allowing faith to guide and strengthen the relationship through mutual beliefs and values.

**Pray and Reflect Together:** Engaging in prayer and reflection as a couple aligns your spiritual goals and nurtures a deeper connection to each other and your shared faith.

**Faith as a Foundation:** Using faith as the foundation of your relationship offers stability and guidance, helping you navigate life's complexities with a shared spiritual perspective.

**Spiritual Growth Enhances Bonding:** Actively seeking spiritual growth together deepens your bond as you support each other in becoming the best versions of yourselves.

**Align Spiritual Values:** Aligning spiritual values ensures harmony in decision-making and strengthens your commitment to a shared path in life.

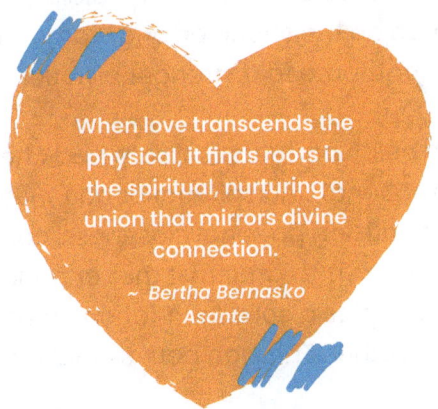

When love transcends the physical, it finds roots in the spiritual, nurturing a union that mirrors divine connection.

~ Bertha Bernasko Asante

## Physical Intimacy

Physical intimacy is a vital component of a healthy and thriving relationship, encompassing both sexual and non-sexual forms of physical affection. While it is not the sole determinant of a strong partnership, it plays a crucial role in fostering a sense of security, closeness, and connection between partners.

Whereas physical intimacy is not the only component, it is a significant part of a relationship. It includes not just erotic connection but also non-sensual physical affection, such as hugging, kissing, and holding hands. Physical intimacy fosters a sense of security and closeness, reinforcing the emotional and spiritual bonds.

Sexual intimacy is an important aspect of physical intimacy, allowing partners to express their love and desire for one another in a way that is both personal and unique. It is an intimate act that can enhance emotional bonds and contribute to a deeper understanding and appreciation of each other. However, physical intimacy extends beyond sexual interaction to include everyday gestures of affection, such as hugging, kissing, and holding hands.

Non-sexual physical touch is equally significant in building and maintaining intimacy. These simple acts of affection convey love, comfort, and support, creating a reassuring environment where both partners feel valued and cared for. Holding hands during a walk, a gentle touch on the shoulder, or a warm embrace after a long day can all contribute to a stronger emotional connection.

Physical intimacy helps partners feel safe and cherished, reinforcing the emotional and spiritual bonds within the relationship. By prioritising physical closeness, couples can cultivate a sense of warmth and trust that enhances their partnership and provides a solid foundation for navigating life's challenges together. Through both sexual and non-sexual expressions of love, physical intimacy nurtures a lasting and fulfilling connection.

## Practicalities of Physical Intimacy
Let us study the situation of a couple regarding their pursuit of building physical intimacy.

My clients, Sam and Rachel, have been married for seven years. They love each other deeply but realised that their physical intimacy had declined over the years.

## Wrong Practice
Sam and Rachel often went to bed at separate times and rarely engaged in physical affection beyond a quick kiss or hug. Their busy schedules and focus on other priorities led to a lack of physical closeness.

My recommended best practice for their implementation:

## Guidance:
**Regular Physical Affection:** They were encouraged to incorporate non-sexual physical affection into their daily routine, such as holding hands, hugging, and cuddling.

**Rekindling Sexual Connection:** They were advised to make time for sexual intimacy, ensuring that it was a priority in their relationship.

**Physical Closeness:** They practiced spending time in close physical proximity, such as sitting close together while watching TV or holding hands during walks.

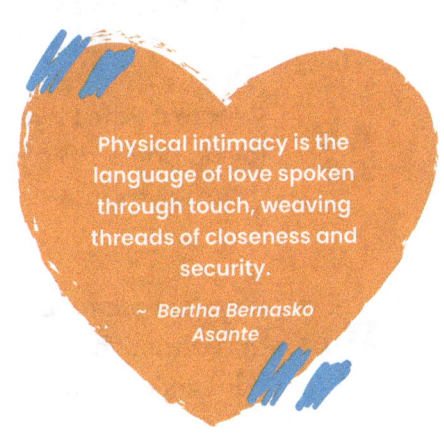

> Physical intimacy is the language of love spoken through touch, weaving threads of closeness and security.
>
> ~ Bertha Bernasko Asante

### Implementation:

Sam and Rachel started a routine of going to bed at the same time, ensuring they had time to cuddle and talk before sleeping. They tried to hold hands and hug more frequently throughout the day. They also scheduled regular date nights that included time for sexual intimacy, ensuring it was a priority.

### Fruitful Outcome:

These practices rekindled Sam and Rachel's physical intimacy, fostering a sense of security and closeness in their relationship. Their increased physical affection reinforced their emotional and spiritual bonds, making their relationship more fulfilling and resilient.

### Wisdom Nuggets for Emotional Intimacy

**Beyond the Physical:** Physical intimacy is more than just sexual expression; it encompasses all forms of touch that convey love and affection, enhancing emotional bonds.

**Touch as a Love Language:** Understanding and appreciating touch as a love language fosters closeness and helps partners feel cherished and connected.

**Create a Safe Physical Space:** Creating a safe and loving physical space allows couples to express themselves freely, nurturing trust and affection.

**Physical presence matters:** Being physically present and attentive to each other's needs strengthens your connection and reinforces the bond between partners.

# CH 3: Exploring Imensions Of Intimacy In Cleaving    *Cleaving To Climax*

**Express Love Physically:** Regularly expressing love through physical gestures, like hugs and kisses, maintains the warmth and affection in your relationship.

## Recreational Intimacy:

Recreational intimacy is an essential aspect of a fulfilling relationship that involves sharing leisure activities and hobbies with your partner. This form of intimacy is centred around the idea that play, adventure, and shared enjoyment can significantly enhance the bond between partners, creating lasting memories and fostering a sense of unity. Recreational intimacy is not just about spending time together; it is about actively engaging in activities that bring joy and excitement, allowing couples to connect on a deeper level through shared experiences.

> Beyond words, physical affection communicates the warmth and comfort that sustain and enrich the marital bond.
> ~ Bertha Bernasko Asante

Participating in recreational activities together allows couples to step outside the routine of daily life and explore new interests, which can reignite passion and enthusiasm in the relationship. Whether it is hiking, travelling, dancing, playing sports, or even engaging in board games, these activities provide opportunities for partners to learn more about each other's preferences, strengths, and quirks. Such shared experiences help build a strong foundation of friendship, which is crucial for enduring love and companionship.

Moreover, recreational intimacy encourages partners to be present and mindful with each other, fostering communication and teamwork. It provides a platform for partners to support and motivate each other, celebrating successes and overcoming challenges together. This sense of partnership and collaboration strengthens the emotional connection and enhances the overall quality of the relationship.

By prioritising recreational intimacy, couples can maintain a sense of fun and adventure in their relationship, keeping it dynamic and vibrant. This shared enjoyment not only enriches the relationship with happiness and laughter but also helps couples navigate the stresses and demands of life, creating a resilient and joyful partnership that thrives on mutual enjoyment and discovery.

> Through shared experiences, couples create lasting memories that strengthen their bond and bring vibrant energy to their relationship.
>
> ~ Bertha Bernasko Asante

## Practicalities of Physical Intimacy

Let us review the conditions of a couple regarding their pursuit of building recreational intimacy.

My clients, Tom and Emily, have been married for eight years. While they love each other deeply, their busy schedules have left them with little time to enjoy recreational activities together. This has led to a feeling of distance and routine in their relationship.

## Wrong Practice

Tom and Emily spend their free time separately—Tom plays video games while Emily attends yoga classes. They rarely plan activities that they can enjoy together, leading to a lack of shared experiences and diminishing their sense of connection.

My recommended Best Practice for Implementation:

## Guidance:

**Shared Hobbies and Activities:** They were encouraged to identify and engage in hobbies and activities that both enjoy.

**Scheduled Leisure Time:** They set aside regular time each week dedicated to recreational activities as a couple.

**Exploration and Experimentation:** They were advised to try new activities together to keep their shared experiences fresh and exciting.

## Implementation:

Tom and Emily began exploring activities they both found enjoyable. They started hiking on weekends, cooking new recipes together, and attending dance classes. They also scheduled a weekly "fun night" where they would try something new, such as visiting a new restaurant or playing a board game.

## Fruitful Outcome

These practices significantly strengthened Tom and Emily's recreational intimacy. They created a reservoir of shared experiences and memories that brought joy and laughter into their relationship. Their bond deepened as they discovered new facets of each other through these activities, leading to a more dynamic and enjoyable partnership.

## Wisdom Nuggets for Recreational Intimacy

 **Play Together, Stay Together:** Engaging in leisure activities and hobbies together strengthens your bond by creating shared experiences and joyful memories.

 **Discover New Interests:** Exploring new recreational activities as a couple keeps your relationship exciting and fosters a sense of adventure and discovery.

 **Balance Work and Play:** Balancing responsibilities with fun ensures a well-rounded relationship that values both achievement and enjoyment.

 **Create lasting memories:** Shared leisure experiences create lasting memories that enhance your bond and provide a foundation of happiness.

 **Foster Joy and Laughter :** Embracing playfulness and laughter in your relationship nurtures a positive atmosphere and deepens your connection.

# CH 3: Exploring Imensions Of Intimacy In Cleaving

## Relational Intimacy

Relational intimacy is a fundamental aspect of a strong and enduring marriage, centred around building a deep friendship between partners. It involves the mutual support, trust, and companionship that form the backbone of any meaningful relationship. By cultivating a strong friendship, couples create a solid foundation for their marriage, allowing them to navigate life's challenges and joys together with greater ease and resilience.

> Shared adventures and laughter lay the groundwork for recreational intimacy, where joy becomes a common language.
>
> ~ Bertha Bernasko Asante

At its core, relational intimacy is about genuinely enjoying each other's company and valuing the time spent together. It requires partners to prioritise quality time, actively listening to each other, and engaging in meaningful conversations. This creates an environment where both individuals feel seen, heard, and appreciated, fostering a sense of emotional safety and connection.

Relational intimacy also involves supporting each other's personal growth and development. By encouraging and celebrating each other's achievements and aspirations, partners can strengthen their bond and build a relationship based on mutual respect and admiration. This support enhances trust and loyalty, key components of a lasting partnership.

> Couples who explore together strengthen bonds through fun.
>
> ~ Bertha Bernasko Asante

Moreover, relational intimacy involves sharing values and life goals, aligning on what matters most to both partners. By working together towards common objectives, couples can experience a sense of unity and purpose that enhances their relationship. Relational intimacy fosters a deep, abiding friendship that enriches the marriage with warmth, love, and companionship, ensuring a dynamic and satisfying relationship that can withstand the test of time.

## Practicalities of Building Relational Intimacy

Let us review the conditions of a couple regarding their pursuit of building recreational intimacy.

**My clients,** James and Lily, have been married for four years. While they have a good marriage, they realised that their relationship lacks the depth of a strong friendship.

## Wrong Practice

James and Lily focus mostly on their roles as partners and parents, often neglecting the aspect of being best friends. They rarely spend time just enjoying each other's company or supporting each other's personal growth outside of their marital roles.

3.6b: My Recommended Best Practice for Implementation:

## Guidance:

**Building Friendship:** They were encouraged to focus on building a friendship by spending quality time together and enjoying each other's company.

**Supporting Personal Growth:** They made efforts to support each other's individual goals and interests, showing genuine interest and encouragement.

**Frequent Communication:** They were advised to communicate regularly about their personal lives, dreams, and interests, not just marital and family responsibilities.

### Implementation:
James and Lily started having regular "friendship dates," where they did activities they both enjoyed without discussing household chores or responsibilities. They showed interest in each other's hobbies—James attended Lily's art exhibits, and Lily supported James in his marathon training. They also began sharing their personal goals and dreams during their evening walks, fostering a deeper understanding and support for each other.

### Fruitful Outcome:
These practices enriched James and Lily's relational intimacy. They became best friends who genuinely enjoyed each other's company and supported each other's personal growth. This foundation of friendship added a new layer of depth and satisfaction to their marriage, making their relationship more resilient and fulfilling.

> Building a strong friendship within marriage forms the basis for relational intimacy, where partners become each other's greatest allies.
>
> ~ Bertha Bernasko Asante

## Wisdom Nuggets for Recreational Intimacy

**Friendship is the Foundation:** A strong friendship forms the bedrock of relational intimacy, where partners genuinely enjoy each other's company and support personal growth.

**Be Best Friends First:** Prioritising friendship ensures that your relationship is built on mutual respect, understanding, and shared interests.

**Support Each Other's Dreams:** Encouraging each other's personal growth and dreams strengthens your bond and fosters a supportive and nurturing relationship.

**Enjoy Each Other's Company:** Spending quality time together as friends reinforces your connection and deepens your relational intimacy.

**Build a Life Together:** Building a shared life with common goals and aspirations enhances your relational intimacy and ensures a lasting partnership.

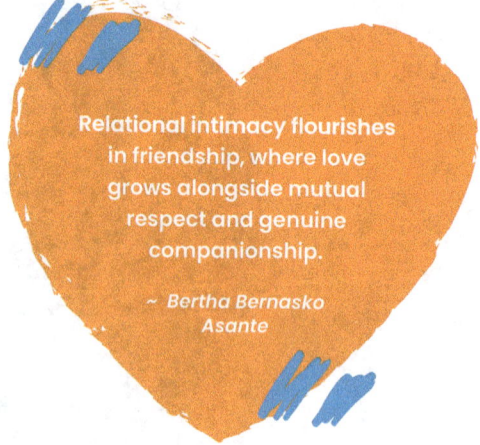

*Relational intimacy flourishes in friendship, where love grows alongside mutual respect and genuine companionship.*

~ Bertha Bernasko Asante

## CHAPTER 4
# CAN A MARRIAGE SURVIVE WITHOUT INTIMACY?

While some marriages may navigate periods of reduced intimacy due to life circumstances or temporary challenges, prolonged lack of intimacy without efforts to address it can strain the relationship significantly. The ability of a marriage to survive without intimacy depends on the willingness of both partners to work towards restoring connection and closeness in meaningful ways.

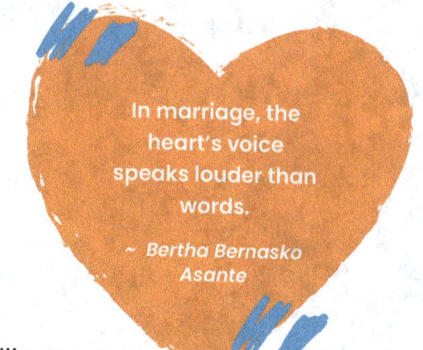

In marriage, the heart's voice speaks louder than words.

~ Bertha Bernasko Asante

## Whether a marriage can survive without intimacy depends on several factors:

**Communication and Willingness to Address Issues:** Couples who are willing to communicate openly, seek help if needed, and work together to address intimacy issues have a better chance of navigating challenges.

**Seeking Professional Help:** Marriage counselling or therapy can provide tools and strategies to improve intimacy and address underlying issues.

**Commitment to the Relationship:** Both partners must be committed to the marriage and willing to invest time and effort into rebuilding intimacy.

The question of whether a marriage can survive without intimacy is complex and multifaceted, as intimacy encompasses various dimensions, including emotional, physical, spiritual, and relational aspects. Here are some considerations regarding the impact of lacking intimacy in a marriage:

## Emotional impact

**Feelings of Disconnection:** A lack of emotional intimacy can lead to feelings of loneliness, isolation, and a sense of not being understood or valued by one's spouse.

**Communication breakdown:** emotional intimacy often involves open and honest communication. Without it, couples may struggle to resolve conflicts, express needs, or support each other effectively.

**Resentment and frustration:** Over time, unresolved emotional issues and unmet needs can breed anger and frustration, creating distance between spouses.

### The Practicalities of Emotional Disconnection:
**What Went Wrong?**

**Couple:** Sarah and Mark have been married for six years. Over time, they have become emotionally distant due to busy work schedules and parenting responsibilities. They rarely are available to talk about their feelings or support each other emotionally, leading to a lack of emotional intimacy.

**Issue:** Both partners feel misunderstood and unappreciated, leading to a growing sense of loneliness and disconnect.

### Best Recommended Practice:
**Open Communication:** Sarah and Mark start by setting aside time each week for uninterrupted, honest conversations about their feelings, dreams, and struggles.

**Emotional Check-ins:** They practice regular emotional check-ins, where each partner shares their current emotional state and listens actively to the other.

**Quality Time:** The couple commits to spending quality time together, engaging in activities that foster emotional connection and empathy.

### Positive Impact of Best Practice:

**Reconnection:** Sarah and Mark feel more emotionally connected and valued by each other.

**Increased Understanding:** Open communication fosters empathy and understanding, allowing them to support each other more effectively.

**Enhanced Trust:** Regular emotional check-ins build trust, reducing feelings of loneliness and isolation.

### Wisdom Nuggets:

 Communication is the bridge that connects hearts in a marriage.

 Openly sharing feelings fosters trust and understanding between partners.

 Quality time together nurtures emotional intimacy and strengthens bonds.

 Listening actively to your partner is a profound act of love.

 Emotional intimacy requires consistent effort and vulnerability.

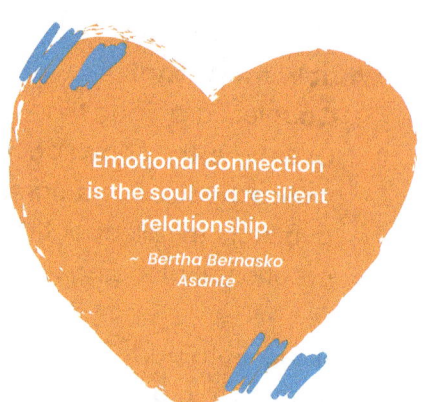

Emotional connection is the soul of a resilient relationship.
~ Bertha Bernasko Asante

## Physical Impact:

**Sexual Frustration:** Physical intimacy is a natural and important aspect of marital bonding. Without it, one or both partners may feel sexually frustrated or unfulfilled.

**Loss of Connection:** Physical affection such as hugging, kissing, and cuddling plays a role in maintaining a sense of closeness and connection between spouses.

**Health Consequences:** Long-term lack of physical intimacy can affect mental and physical health, potentially leading to stress, anxiety, and even issues such as depression.

### Scenario: Lack of Physical Intimacy:

**What Went Wrong?**

**Couple:** John and Lisa have been married for eight years. Due to hectic work schedules and parenting duties, they rarely engage in physical affection, resulting in a lack of physical intimacy.

**Issue:** Both partners feel sexually frustrated and disconnected, impacting their overall relationship satisfaction.

### Best Recommended Practice:

**Prioritise Physical Intimacy:** John and Lisa schedule regular date nights and set aside time for physical affection, such as hugging, kissing, and cuddling.

**Open Discussion:** They discuss their physical needs and desires openly, ensuring that both feel respected and valued.

**Create a Romantic Environment:** The couple makes efforts to create a romantic environment at home, fostering an atmosphere conducive to physical connection.

## Positive Impact of Best Practice:

**Renewed Closeness:** John and Lisa feel closer and more connected, both physically and emotionally.

**Increased Satisfaction:** Regular physical intimacy improves relationship satisfaction and strengthens their bond.

**Reduced Stress:** Physical affection helps reduce stress and enhances overall well-being for both partners.

## Wisdom Nuggets:

Physical intimacy is the language of love spoken through touch.

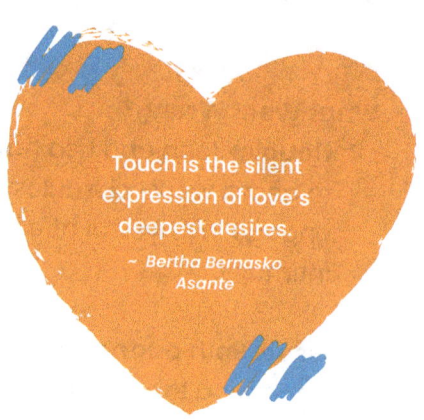
*Touch is the silent expression of love's deepest desires.*
~ Bertha Bernasko Asante

Prioritising affection strengthens the bond between partners.

Open discussions about needs foster mutual respect and understanding.

Creating a romantic environment nurtures intimacy and connection.

Regular physical closeness enhances relationship satisfaction.

## Spiritual Impact:

**Diminished Spiritual Connection:** For couples who share spiritual beliefs, intimacy can involve praying together, sharing faith experiences, and growing spiritually as a couple.

**Impact on Values and Morals:** Intimacy often reinforces shared values and morals within the context of marriage. A lack of intimacy may strain these shared foundations.

**Health Consequences:** Long-term lack of physical intimacy can affect mental and physical health, potentially leading to stress, anxiety, and even issues such as depression.

### Scenario: Diminished Spiritual Connection
**What Went Wrong?**

**Couple:** Alex and Nina have been married for seven years. They have neglected the spiritual aspect of their relationship, leading to a diminished sense of spiritual connection.

**Issue:** Both partners feel disconnected from each other spiritually and struggle to find shared meaning and purpose.

### Best Recommended Practice:

**Joint Spiritual Activities:** Alex and Nina engage in joint spiritual activities, such as attending religious services together or participating in spiritual retreats.

**Shared Values:** They discuss and align their spiritual values and beliefs, creating a shared sense of purpose.

**Prayer and Reflection:** The couple incorporates prayer and reflection into their daily routine, fostering a deeper spiritual connection.

### Positive Impact of Best Practice:

**Enhanced Spiritual Bond:** Alex and Nina feel more connected spiritually, enriching their relationship with shared meaning and purpose.

**Stronger Values:** Aligning their values strengthens their relationship's foundation and reinforces shared morals.

**Renewed Purpose:** Joint spiritual activities provide a renewed sense of purpose and direction in their marriage.

### Wisdom Nuggets:

 Joint spiritual activities nurture a deep connection in marriage.

 Shared values strengthen the foundation of a relationship.

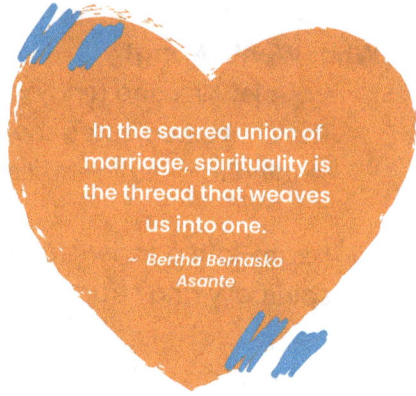

*In the sacred union of marriage, spirituality is the thread that weaves us into one.*
~ Bertha Bernasko Asante

 Prayer and reflection deepen the spiritual bond between partners.

 Aligning beliefs creates a shared sense of purpose and direction.

 In marriage, spiritual intimacy is the compass that guides us together.

## Relational Impact:

**Decreased Relationship Satisfaction:** Intimacy fosters a sense of partnership and mutual support. Without it, couples may feel less satisfied with their relationship overall.

**Increased Risk of Infidelity:** Lack of intimacy can sometimes lead to one or both partners seeking emotional or physical connection outside the marriage, increasing the risk of infidelity.

**Parenting Challenges:** Intimacy in marriage can model healthy relationships for children. A lack of intimacy may impact parenting dynamics and family cohesion.

### Practicalities of Decreased Relationship Satisfaction

**What Went Wrong?**

  **Couple:** Tom and Mia have been married for ten years. Over time, they have focused more on their individual careers and less on nurturing their relationships, leading to decreased satisfaction and partnership.

  **Issue:** Both partners feel distant and unsupported, resulting in a lack of mutual support and partnership.

### Best Recommended Practice:

**Mutual Support:** Tom and Mia prioritise supporting each other's goals and aspirations, celebrating achievements, and offering encouragement during challenges.

**Shared Goals:** They set shared goals and work towards them together, fostering a sense of partnership and teamwork.

**Regular Check-ins:** The couple establishes regular relationship check-ins to discuss their satisfaction levels and address any concerns.

### Positive Impact of Best Practice:

**Strengthened Partnership:** Tom and Mia feel more supported and valued, enhancing their sense of partnership.

**Increased Satisfaction:** Working towards shared goals increases relationship satisfaction and strengthens their bond.

**Improved Communication:** Regular check-ins encourage open communication and prevent issues from escalating.

### Wisdom Nuggets:

Supporting each other's dreams nurtures a strong partnership.

Shared goals strengthen the bond and foster teamwork.

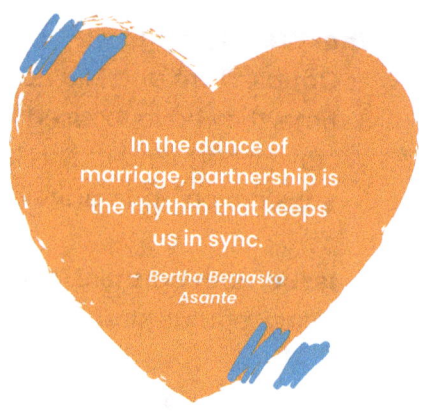

*In the dance of marriage, partnership is the rhythm that keeps us in sync.*

~ Bertha Bernasko Asante

Regular check-ins ensure relationship satisfaction and growth.

Celebrating achievements together deepens mutual respect and admiration.

In marriage, teamwork transforms dreams into reality.

## Cultural and Personal Factors:

**Cultural norms and expectations:** Cultural factors can influence how intimacy is perceived and valued within a marriage.

**Personal Differences:** Individual preferences and comfort levels regarding intimacy can vary. Understanding and respecting these differences is crucial in navigating intimacy challenges.

**The Practicalities of Navigating Personal Differences**

### Practicalities of Decreased Relationship Satisfaction
**What Went Wrong?**
    **Couple:** Leo and Lisa have been married for five years. They come from unfamiliar cultural backgrounds, which has led to misunderstandings and disagreements about the role of intimacy in their marriage.

    **Issue:** Cultural norms and personal differences have created tension, leading to a lack of intimacy and connection.

### Best Recommended Practice:
**Cultural Understanding:** Leo and Lisa take time to learn about and respect each other's cultural backgrounds and traditions, fostering empathy and understanding.

**Personal Preferences:** They communicate openly about their personal preferences and comfort levels regarding intimacy, finding common ground that respects both partners' needs.

**Compromise and Adaptation:** The couple practices compromise and adapts their approach to intimacy, creating a balance that honours both cultural and personal factors.

## Positive Impact of Best Practice:

**Enhanced Understanding:** Leo and Lisa gain a deeper appreciation for each other's backgrounds and perspectives, reducing misunderstandings.

**Increased Empathy:** Open communication and compromise promote empathy, strengthening their emotional bond.

**Harmonious Relationship:** By respecting and valuing each other's differences, they create a harmonious and fulfilling relationship.

## Wisdom Nuggets:

Cultural understanding fosters empathy and strengthens relationships.

Respecting personal preferences nurtures a balanced and fulfilling marriage.

Open communication bridges the gap between cultural and personal differences.

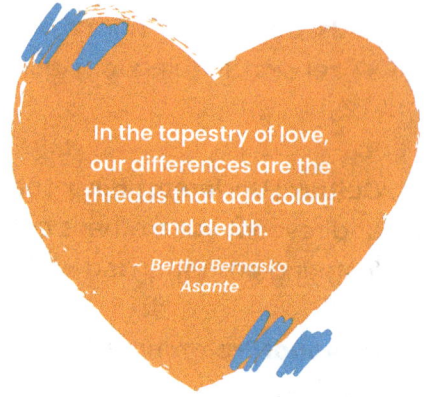
*In the tapestry of love, our differences are the threads that add colour and depth.*
~ Bertha Bernasko Asante

Compromise and adaptation create harmony and connection in marriage.

In marriage, diversity is a source of strength and growth.

# CHAPTER 5
# LONG-DISTANT COUPLES

Long-distance couples, who find themselves physically separated for prolonged periods due to various reasons such as career demands, educational pursuits, or other commitments, face unique challenges that can affect their intimacy on multiple levels. Distance can strain emotional closeness as the inability to be physically present with one's partner may lead to feelings of loneliness, longing, and isolation. Communication becomes paramount in maintaining the emotional connection, but the lack of non-verbal cues and shared experiences can sometimes create misunderstandings or feelings of disconnection. Moreover, the absence of physical touch and intimacy can also pose challenges to the couple's ability to nurture their bond, requiring them to find alternative ways to express affection and remain connected despite the physical distance. Thus, long-distance couples need to proactively navigate these obstacles, prioritize open and honest communication, and cultivate trust and understanding to sustain their intimacy and strengthen their relationship despite the miles that separate them.

> True oneness in marriage is achieved through openness, where vulnerability and acceptance weave a tapestry of trust.
> ~ Bertha Bernasko Asante

## Intimacy challenges with married couples living apart.

**Physical Intimacy Challenges:** Physical intimacy, including sexual intimacy, is naturally limited when spouses are geographically separated. This can lead to frustration and longing for physical closeness.

**Emotional Distance:** Lack of daily face-to-face interaction can create emotional distance between spouses. They may feel disconnected or struggle to maintain emotional intimacy without regular in-person contact.

**Communication Struggles:** Effective communication can be

challenging with distance. Time zone differences, busy schedules, and reliance on technology (phone calls, video chats) can affect the quality and frequency of communication.

**Decreased Shared Experiences:** Couples living apart may miss sharing daily life experiences, which are important for building shared memories and deepening emotional intimacy.

**Impact on Trust:** Distance can sometimes lead to insecurities or doubts about the relationship, particularly if there are communication gaps or limited opportunities to reinforce trust through shared activities and experiences.

**Role Changes:** When one spouse is away, roles within the relationship may shift. This can affect dynamics related to decision-making, household responsibilities, and emotional support.

**Role Changes: Role Changes:** When one spouse is away, roles within the relationship may shift. This can affect dynamics related to decision-making, household responsibilities, and emotional support.

**Sexual and romantic frustration:** Physical separation can lead to sexual frustration and difficulty maintaining a romantic connection. Couples may need to find alternative ways to express affection and maintain sexual intimacy.

## Intimacy Challenges with Married Couples Living Apart:

**Effective Communication:** Prioritise open, honest, and regular communication. Schedule time for meaningful conversations and ensure both spouses feel heard and understood.

**Technology Use:** Utilise technology creatively to stay connected. Video calls, messaging apps, and social media can help bridge the distance and maintain a sense of closeness.

**Quality Time:** When possible, plan visits and spend quality time together. Make the most of the time spent in person to strengthen emotional and physical intimacy.

**Emotional Support:** Offer each other emotional support and encouragement, even from afar. Stay attuned to each other's needs and provide reassurance and comfort when needed.

**Shared Goals and Plans:** Maintain a sense of partnership by discussing and working towards common goals and plans. This can foster a sense of unity and purpose in the relationship.

**Physical Intimacy:** Explore ways to maintain physical intimacy, such as sending thoughtful gifts, writing love letters, or engaging in intimate conversations about desires and fantasies.

Ultimately, maintaining intimacy in a long-distance marriage requires effort, creativity, and a commitment from both spouses to prioritise their relationship despite the physical separation. With intentional communication and nurturing of emotional and physical connections, couples can navigate the challenges of distance and strengthen their bond over time.

# CHAPTER 6
# COMMON MARITAL MISTAKES

**Common mistakes** that can jeopardize a healthy and intimate marriage often arise from misunderstandings, miscommunications, or neglect of essential relationship aspects. Recognising and addressing these pitfalls is crucial for maintaining a strong marital bond. Some of the most frequent errors couples make include failing to prioritise quality time together, allowing unresolved conflicts to fester, neglecting emotional support and connection, taking each other for granted, lacking effective communication, and failing to nurture intimacy and romance. By identifying these common mistakes and proactively working to overcome them, couples can fortify their relationship, deepen their emotional connection, and cultivate a fulfilling and lasting partnership.

## Neglecting Communication:

**Mistake:** Assuming your partner knows your needs, desires, or concerns without expressing them.

**Consequence:** This can lead to misunderstandings, resentment, and emotional distance.

**Solution:** Prioritise open, honest, and regular communication about both the mundane and significant aspects of your relationship.

### Practicalities of Neglecting Communication

**Mistake:** Assuming your partner knows your needs, desires, or concerns without expressing them.

**Scenario:** John assumes that Sarah knows he's stressed from work and doesn't want to talk. Sarah feels ignored and unloved, believing John is pulling away from her. This lack of communication leads to growing tension.

**My recommendation:** To improve, John should express his feelings openly with Sarah, explaining his stress and need for

## CH 6: Common Marital Mistakes

space while reassuring her of his love. Sarah, in turn, should share her feelings of neglect and ask how she can support him during this time.

**Scripture Example:** James 1:19 - "Everyone should be quick to listen, slow to speak and slow to become angry."

## Taking Each Other for Granted:

**Mistake:** Failing to appreciate and acknowledge your partner's efforts and contributions.

**Solution:** Regularly express gratitude and recognise the small and large ways your partner contributes to the relationship.

## Practicalities of Taking Each Other for Granted

**Scenario:** Emma consistently takes care of the household chores, but her husband, David, rarely acknowledges her efforts. Over time, Emma feels unappreciated and begins to resent David.

**My recommendation:** David should take time to notice and verbally appreciate Emma's hard work. A small gesture of thanks or a surprise act of kindness can go a long way in making Emma feel valued.

**Scripture Example:** Ephesians 5:33 - "However, each one of you also must love his wife as he loves himself, and the wife must respect her husband."

## Ignoring Emotional Intimacy:

**Mistake:** Focusing solely on physical intimacy while neglecting the emotional connection.

**Consequence:** This can lead to a lack of fulfilment and a feeling of distance in the relationship.

**Solution:** Invest time in building emotional intimacy through meaningful conversations, shared experiences, and empathy.

**Scenario:** Lisa and Mark have a regular physical relationship, but they rarely talk about their deeper feelings or personal struggles. Over time, they feel disconnected emotionally, even though they are physically close.

**My recommendation:** They should set aside time for heart-to-heart conversations where they can share their fears, dreams, and experiences. Engaging in activities that build emotional connection, like praying or reading together, can deepen their emotional intimacy.

**Scripture Example:** 1 Peter 3:8 - "Finally, all of you, be like-minded, be sympathetic, love one another, be compassionate and humble."

## Letting Conflicts Escalate:

**Mistake:** Allowing small disagreements to grow into larger conflicts by not addressing them promptly.

**Consequence:** This can create ongoing tension and unresolved issues.

**Solution:** Address conflicts early, seek to understand each other's perspectives, and work together to find resolutions.

**Scenario:** After a small disagreement about finances, Adam and Rachel stop talking for days, letting the issue fester. The silence turns into a bigger conflict, causing significant strain on their relationship.

**My recommendation:** They should address issues as they arise, approaching each other with love and a willingness to listen. Seeking resolution through calm, constructive dialogue is essential.

**Scripture Example:** Ephesians 4:26 - "In your anger do not sin: Do not let the sun go down while you are still angry."

## Neglecting Physical Intimacy:

**Mistake:** Allowing the demands of daily life to overshadow the importance of physical closeness.

**Consequence:** This can lead to a lack of connection and dissatisfaction in the marriage.

**Solution:** Prioritise physical intimacy, even if it means scheduling time for it, to maintain a strong bond.

**Scenario:** Laura and Mike are so busy with work, children, and other responsibilities that they haven't made time for physical intimacy. They start feeling like roommates rather than a married couple.

**My recommendation:** They should schedule regular date nights or intimate time together, prioritising their physical connection just as much as other aspects of their relationship.

**Scripture Example:**
*"The husband should fulfil his marital duty to his wife, and likewise the wife to her husband."*

## Not Setting Boundaries with Others:

**Mistake:** Allowing outside influences, including family and friends, to interfere with the marriage.

**Consequence:** This can create tension and conflict within the relationship.

**Solution:** Establish and maintain healthy boundaries to protect your marriage and prioritise your partner.

**Scenario:** Abena's parents constantly interfere in her marriage with Tim, giving unsolicited advice and criticising Tim's decisions. This causes tension between Abena and Tim.

**My recommendation:** Abena and Tim should set clear boundaries with her parents, politely but firmly explaining that their marriage decisions are private. This will protect their relationship from external stress.

**Scripture Example:** Genesis 2:24 - "That is why a man leaves his father and mother and is united to his wife, and they become one flesh."

## Failing to Invest in the Relationship:

**Mistake:** Believing that love alone is enough without continued effort.

**Consequence:** This can lead to stagnation and a loss of connection over time.

**Solution:** Continuously invest in the relationship by spending quality time together, learning new things about each other, and growing together.

**Scenario:** Steve and Ola have been married for years and no longer make time for each other, assuming their love is strong enough without much effort. They grow distant and feel more like roommates than partners.

**My recommendation:** They should actively invest in their relationship by trying new activities together, revisiting places with special memories, and continuing to learn about each other's evolving interests.

**Scripture Example:** Proverbs 5:18-19 - "May your fountain be blessed, and may you rejoice in the wife of your youth."

## Overlooking Spiritual Connection:

**Mistake:** Ignoring the spiritual aspect of the relationship, especially if it is important to both partners.

**Consequence:** This can lead to a lack of deeper connection and shared values.

**Solution:** Engage in spiritual practices together, such as praying, attending religious services, or discussing your faith.

**Scenario:** Osei and Jessica rarely pray together or discuss their faith, even though they both value their spiritual beliefs. Their spiritual lives become separate, weakening their overall connection.

**My recommendation:** They should make time for shared spiritual practices, like praying, attending church, or reading scripture together. This will help them grow closer to each other and to God.

**Scripture Example:** Matthew 18:20 - "For where two or three gather in my name, there am I with them."

## Resisting Change and Growth:

**Mistake:** Expecting your partner to remain the same over time and resisting changes in the relationship.

**Consequence:** This can cause frustration and a feeling of being stuck in the relationship.

**Solution:** Embrace growth and change, understanding that both partners will evolve, and the relationship must adapt accordingly.

**Scenario:** Maria expects her husband, James, to stay the same person he was when they married. As he grows and changes, she resists, feeling that the changes are pulling them apart.

**My recommendation:** Maria should embrace and support James's growth, understanding that change is natural and can strengthen their relationship. They should openly discuss their individual growth and how to adapt as a couple.

**Scripture Example:** Philippians 1:9 - "And this is my prayer: that your love may abound more and more in knowledge and depth of insight."

## Comparing Your Relationship to Others:

**Mistake:** Measuring your relationship against others, especially based on social media or superficial observations.

**Consequence:** This can lead to unrealistic expectations and dissatisfaction.

**Solution:** Focus on your unique relationship, appreciate its strengths, and work on areas of improvement without comparing it to others.

**Scenario:** Karen frequently compares her marriage to the seemingly perfect relationships she sees on social media. She becomes dissatisfied with her own marriage, focusing on its flaws rather than its strengths.

**My recommendation:** Karen should focus on the unique strengths and qualities of her own marriage, appreciating what makes her relationship special. Avoiding comparisons helps to maintain contentment and gratitude.

**Scripture Example:** Galatians 6:4 - "Each one should test their own actions. Then they can take pride in themselves alone, without comparing themselves to someone else."

By being aware of these common mistakes and actively working to avoid them, you can nurture a healthier, more intimate, and fulfilling marriage.

## CHAPTER 7

# PRACTICAL TIPS AND BIBLICAL INSIGHTS FOR ADDRESSING COMMON MARITAL MISTAKES

By addressing these scenarios with the recommended practices and grounding them in biblical principles, couples can foster healthier, more fulfilling relationships.

## Prioritise Quality Time

**Tip:** Make a deliberate effort to spend quality time together, even if it's just a few minutes each day. This strengthens your bond and ensures you stay connected in the midst of busy lives.

**Biblical Insight:** Ecclesiastes 4:9-10 - "Two are better than one... If either of them falls down, one can help the other up."

## Practice Forgiveness

**Tip:** Be quick to forgive and let go of grudges. Holding onto resentment can create distance in your relationship.

**Biblical Insight:** Ephesians 4:32 - "Be kind and compassionate to one another, forgiving each other, just as in Christ God forgave you."

## Show Appreciation Regularly

**Tip:** Regularly express gratitude for your spouse, whether it's for small daily tasks or larger efforts. This fosters a positive atmosphere and encourages mutual respect.

**Biblical Insight:** 1 Thessalonians 5:18 - "Give thanks in all circumstances; for this is God's will for you in Christ Jesus."

## Be Intentional with Affection

**Tip:** Show physical affection often—whether through hugs, kisses, or holding hands. Physical touch is a powerful way to express love and closeness.

**Biblical Insight:** Song of Solomon 1:2 - "Let him kiss me with the kisses of his mouth— for your love is more delightful than wine."

## Keep Humour Alive

**Tip:** Don't underestimate the power of laughter. Sharing light moments and humour can relieve stress and keep your relationship joyful.

**Biblical Insight:** Proverbs 17:22 - "A cheerful heart is good medicine, but a crushed spirit dries up the bones."

## Be Each Other's Biggest Supporter

**Tip:** Cheer on your spouse's goals, dreams, and efforts. Be their strongest ally and biggest fan in all aspects of life.

**Biblical Insight:** Romans 12:10 - "Be devoted to one another in love. Honor one another above yourselves."

## Continue Dating Each Other

**Tip:** Keep the romance alive by continuing to date each other, even after years of marriage. Plan regular dates that allow you to connect and enjoy each other's company.

**Biblical Insight:** Proverbs 5:18 - "May your fountain be blessed, and may you rejoice in the wife of your youth."

## Maintain a Shared Vision

**Tip:** Regularly discuss your shared goals, values, and dreams. Having a unified vision for your future strengthens your bond and ensures you're moving in the same direction.

**Biblical Insight:** Amos 3:3 - "Do two walk together unless they have agreed to do so?"

## Embrace Vulnerability

**Tip:** Don't be afraid to be vulnerable with each other. Sharing your fears, weaknesses, and hopes can deepen your connection and build trust.

**Biblical Insight:** 2 Corinthians 12:9 - "But he said to me, 'My grace is sufficient for you, for my power is made perfect in weakness.' Therefore, I will boast all the more gladly about my weaknesses, so that Christ's power may rest on me."

## Pray Together

**Tip:** Make praying together a regular practice. It does not only bring you closer to God but also to each other, creating a spiritual bond that fortifies your marriage.

**Biblical Insight:** Matthew 18:19 - "Again, truly I tell you that if two of you on earth agree about anything they ask for, it will be done for them by my Father in heaven."

# CHAPTER 8
# THE LIVING WORD ON CLEAVING AND INTIMACY

The teachings of The Living Word offer profound insights into the essence of intimacy within marriage, emphasising its sacred nature, shared responsibility, and spiritual depth. These scriptures underscore the significance of cleaving in a marriage, encouraging partners to come together not only physically but also spiritually, cherishing and upholding the sanctity of their union. The emphasis on unity and mutual respect in these teachings serves as a guiding principle for couples seeking to deepen their connection and build a strong foundation for their relationship. By embracing these foundational values, couples can nurture a bond that is not only rooted in love and understanding but also enriched by the spiritual dimensions of their commitment to each other.

> In the sacred union of marriage, two become one, mirroring the divine harmony that guides us in love.
>
> ~ Bertha Bernasko Asante

## Intimacy and Oneness

Genesis 2:24-25 *"Therefore, a man shall leave his father and his mother and hold fast to his wife, and they shall become one flesh. And the man and his wife were both naked and were not ashamed."*

This passage from Genesis lays the foundation for marital intimacy, illustrating the intended unity between husband and wife. It emphasises that a couple should leave their parents to form a new and independent unit, both physically and spiritually. The reference to being "naked and not ashamed" symbolises a state of complete openness and vulnerability, highlighting the deep trust and acceptance that should exist between partners.

### Practical scenario:

**Couple: Bill and Vera** have been married for two years and are struggling to find balance in their relationship with their families.

They often turn to their parents for advice, which sometimes leads to conflicts and misunderstandings in their marriage.

**Guidance and implementation:** To strengthen their marriage, Bill and Vera were counselled to set boundaries with their parents and prioritise their relationship. They start a weekly routine where they openly share their feelings and thoughts with each other, creating a safe space for vulnerability. They also make decisions together without outside influence, reinforcing their unity as a couple.

**Outcome:** By prioritising their relationship and embracing openness, Bill and Vera cultivate a deeper sense of trust and oneness. Their bond becomes more resilient, enabling them to navigate challenges together.

### Wisdom Nuggets for Intimacy and Oneness

The nuggets below emphasise the importance of prioritising the couple's relationship, advancing open communication, and establishing boundaries to create a strong and lasting union.

**Create Boundaries to Foster Independence:** Setting healthy boundaries with family members allows couples to develop their unique identity and strengthens their commitment to each other. Independence from outside influence is essential for nurturing a strong marital foundation.

**Practice Vulnerability to Build Trust:** Regularly sharing feelings and thoughts in a safe, non-judgemental space helps partners understand and appreciate each other's perspectives. This openness fosters trust and deepens the emotional connection between spouses.

**Prioritise Your Relationship Above External Influences:** Decisions made as a couple should prioritise the partnership over external opinions. Embracing unity in decision-making reinforces the couple's commitment to each other and strengthens their bond.

**Cultivate Openness to Enhance Understanding:** Embracing complete openness and honesty allows partners to fully understand and accept each other, fostering a deeper connection. This mutual understanding forms the basis for a supportive and loving relationship.

**Celebrate Individuality Within the Union:** While striving for unity, it is essential to appreciate and celebrate each partner's individuality. Recognising each other's unique strengths and perspectives enriches the relationship and supports a harmonious balance.

> True oneness in marriage is achieved through openness, where vulnerability and acceptance weave a tapestry of trust.
>
> ~ Bertha Bernasko Asante

## Mutual Responsibility in Physical Intimacy

**Corinthians 7:3-5:** *"The husband should give to his wife her conjugal rights, and likewise the wife to her husband. The wife does not have authority over her own body, but the husband does. Likewise, the husband does not have authority over his own body, but the wife does. Do not deprive one another, except perhaps by agreement for a limited time, that you may devote yourselves to prayer; but then come together again, so that Satan may not tempt you because of your lack of self-control."*

This passage emphasises the mutual responsibility spouses have towards each other in the realm of physical intimacy. It teaches that marriage involves a partnership where both husband and wife have equal authority over each other's bodies, reinforcing the idea of mutual respect and consent. Temporary abstinence from physical intimacy is allowed only by mutual agreement and for a specific purpose, underscoring the importance of regular physical connection to maintain the strength of the marital bond and avoid temptation.

### Practical scenario:

**Couple:** Daniel and Emma have been married for five years. Recently, they have been experiencing a lack of intimacy due to their demanding work schedules and family responsibilities.

**Guidance and implementation:** Daniel and Emma decide to prioritise their physical intimacy by scheduling regular date nights and setting aside time for each other. They discuss their needs and desires openly, ensuring that both feel valued and respected. They also agree on a temporary break from intimacy when Emma wants to focus on her spiritual growth through prayer, with the understanding that they will reconnect after the agreed period.

**Outcome:** By prioritising their physical intimacy and maintaining open communication, Daniel and Emma strengthen their marital bond. They feel more connected and satisfied, reducing the risk of temptation and enhancing their overall relationship.

### Wisdom Nuggets for Mutual Responsibility in Physical Intimacy

The nuggets below emphasise the importance of prioritising physical intimacy, maintaining open communication, and respecting each other's needs and boundaries to build a strong and fulfilling relationship.

**Prioritise physical intimacy amidst busy schedules:** Even with demanding work and family responsibilities, setting aside dedicated time for physical connection is vital for nurturing the marital bond. Regular date nights or intentional moments together help maintain closeness.

**Communicate openly about needs and desires:** Honest and open discussions about physical intimacy ensure that both partners feel valued, respected, and understood. This communication fosters mutual respect and helps address any issues before they become barriers.

**Respect and consent are essential:** Mutual respect and consent are foundational in any intimate relationship. Understanding that each partner has equal authority over their bodies reinforces the idea of partnership and mutual responsibility.

**Allow for Temporary Abstinence with Mutual Agreement:** Agreeing on temporary breaks from physical intimacy for specific purposes, such as spiritual growth, can be beneficial. It is crucial that both partners are on the same page and have a clear plan for reconnecting.

**Strengthen bonds to reduce temperature:** Regular physical connection and emotional intimacy reduce the risk of outside temptations and strengthen the marital bond. A committed partnership creates a safe and fulfilling environment for both partners.

## Sanctity of Marriage and Intimacy

**Hebrews 13:4:** *"Let marriage be held in honour among all, and let the marriage bed be undefiled, for God will judge the sexually immoral and adulterous."*

> Mutual responsibility in intimacy honours the balance of giving and receiving, nurturing a partnership built on respect.
> ~ Bertha Bernasko Asante

This verse underscores the sanctity of marriage and the purity of intimacy within it. It teaches that sexual relations within marriage are honourable and should be respected, while sexual immorality and adultery are condemned. The verse calls for couples to honour their commitment to each other, maintaining fidelity and purity in their relationship.

**Practical scenario:**
**Couple:** Jessica and Ryan have been married for eight years. Recently, Ryan faced temptation at work due to an attractive colleague, leading to feelings of guilt and unease in his marriage.

**Guidance and implementation:** Jessica and Ryan were counselled to strengthen their marriage by focussing on the sanctity of their commitment. They attend a marriage retreat where they renew their vows and discuss the importance of fidelity. They also establish boundaries with colleagues and focus on building trust and transparency in their relationship.

**Outcome:** By honouring their marriage and maintaining fidelity, Jessica and Ryan enhance their intimacy and trust. Their renewed commitment to each other strengthens their bond, allowing them to navigate challenges with confidence and unity.

*Fidelity is the heart of unity; honour your vows to nurture love's purity.*

~ Bertha Bernasko Asante

## Wisdom Nuggets for Sanctity of Marriage and Intimacy

The nuggets below highlight the importance of honouring marriage, setting boundaries, and maintaining open communication to protect and nurture the sanctity of the marital relationship.

 **Honour Marriage as a Sacred Commitment:** Recognise marriage as a sacred bond that requires mutual respect and dedication. Upholding the sanctity of marriage strengthens the relationship and fosters a deep sense of trust and unity.

 **Establish and respect boundaries:** Setting clear boundaries in social and professional environments helps protect the marriage from outside temptations. Respecting these boundaries reinforces the commitment to fidelity and purity.

**Renew Vows to Reinforce Commitment:** Periodically renewing vows can serve as a powerful reminder of the promises made to each other. It can revitalise the relationship and deepen the emotional and spiritual connection between partners.

**Focus on Building Trust and Transparency:** Open communication and honesty are essential for maintaining trust in a marriage. Sharing feelings and concerns with each other helps address potential issues before they escalate.

**Seek Guidance and Support When Needed:** Participating in marriage retreats or counselling sessions can provide valuable insights and tools for strengthening the marital bond. Seeking support demonstrates a commitment to growth and improvement.

> The sanctity of marriage is upheld through fidelity and purity, where love is celebrated within the bounds of sacred commitment.
>
> ~ Bertha Bernasko Asante

## Celebrating Love and Intimacy

**Song of Solomon (Song of Songs):**
*The Song of Solomon is a poetic book that celebrates the beauty and intimacy of love between a husband and wife. It uses rich and metaphorical language to depict the passionate and exclusive love within marriage.*

The entire book of 'Songs of Solomon' highlights the passionate and joyful aspects of marital love, emphasising that intimacy is a beautiful and God-given gift to be cherished. It encourages couples to appreciate and celebrate each other, fostering a relationship full of delight and admiration. The poetic expressions in the Song of Solomon serve as a reminder of the deep emotional and physical connection that should exist in a marriage.

**Practical scenario:**
**Couple:** Cederick and Rose have been married for three years. They love each other deeply but often find themselves caught up in daily routines, leading to a lack of excitement and romance.

**Guidance and implementation:** Cederick and Rose decide to reignite their passion by taking inspiration from the Song of Solomon. They plan romantic getaways and surprise each other with thoughtful gestures. They also express their love through letters and poems, celebrating each other's unique qualities and beauty.

**Outcome:** By celebrating their love and embracing romance, Cederick and Rose create a vibrant and passionate relationship. Their renewed appreciation for each other deepens their emotional and physical connection, bringing joy and fulfilment to their marriage.

**Wisdom Nuggets for Sanctity of Marriage and Intimacy**
The nuggets below focus on the importance of celebrating love

with intentionality and creativity, nurturing admiration, and appreciation to create a joyful and fulfilling marriage.

**Celebrate Love with Intention:** Intentionally celebrating love keeps the romance alive. Thoughtful gestures, surprises, and romantic getaways can reignite passion and bring excitement to the relationship.

**Express Appreciation and Admiration:** Regularly expressing admiration and appreciation for your partner's qualities strengthens the emotional bond. Verbal affirmations, letters, and poems are powerful tools for conveying love and admiration.

**Prioritise Quality Time Together:** Carving out time for each other amidst daily routines fosters connection and intimacy. Sharing experiences and creating memories strengthen the marital bond.

**Embrace Playfulness and Creativity:** Infusing playfulness and creativity into the relationship keeps it dynamic and fun. Exploring new activities together enhances the sense of adventure and closeness.

**Reflect on the Beauty of Marital Love:** Reflecting on the beauty and joy of marital love deepens appreciation and gratitude. Viewing intimacy as a cherished gift encourages couples to nurture and protect their relationship.

> Marital love is a canvas painted with vibrant expressions of joy and devotion, reflecting the beauty of intimate connection.
>
> ~ Bertha Bernasko Asante

## Unity and the Mystery of Marriage

**Ephesians 5:31-33:** *"Therefore, a man shall leave his father and mother and hold fast to his wife, and the two shall become one flesh." This mystery is profound, and I am saying that it refers to Christ and the church.*

This passage highlights the unity and oneness in marriage, drawing a parallel between the marital relationship and the relationship between Christ and the church. It emphasises the profound nature of marriage as a sacred bond where two individuals become one, reflecting the love and unity that Christ has with the church. The passage encourages couples to strive for a deep spiritual connection, understanding that their union reflects a greater divine mystery.

### Practical scenario:

**Couple:** Emman and Anna have been married for ten years. While they share a strong partnership, they feel disconnected spiritually and are seeking a deeper understanding of their marriage's significance.

**Guidance and implementation:** Emman and Anna decide to explore the spiritual dimension of their marriage by studying the teachings of Ephesians 5:31–33. They attend a couples' Bible study group, where they discuss the parallels between marriage and the relationship between Christ and the church. They also engage in joint prayer and spiritual activities, seeking to deepen their understanding of their union's sacred nature.

**Outcome:** By embracing the spiritual dimension of their marriage, Emman and Anna achieve a profound sense of unity and purpose. They gain a deeper appreciation for their relationship's sacredness, allowing them to support and uplift each other in all aspects of their lives.

The above scenarios demonstrate how couples can apply biblical teachings to cultivate intimacy in their marriages. By prioritising mutual respect, fidelity, romance, and spiritual connection, couples can experience the fullness of intimacy as intended by the Living Word. Through these practices, they can build resilient and fulfilling relationships that honour the sanctity and significance of marriage.

### Wisdom Nuggets for Unity and the Mystery of Marriage

The nuggets below underline the spiritual depth and unity that marriage embodies, encouraging couples to seek a deeper connection that honours the profound nature of their union.

**Embrace the Spiritual Dimension of Marriage:** Understanding marriage as a reflection of the relationship between Christ and the church enriches the spiritual bond between partners, providing a profound sense of unity and purpose.

**Foster Deep Spiritual Connection:** Engaging in joint spiritual activities, such as prayer and Bible study, strengthens the spiritual intimacy between spouses, allowing them to grow together in faith and understanding.

 **Reflect the Sacred Nature of Marriage:** Viewing marriage as a sacred bond encourages couples to honour and cherish their union, recognising its significance in their lives and its reflection of a divine mystery.

 **Seek Unity Through Understanding:** Striking for unity involves deepening mutual understanding and respect, aligning values and goals to support each other in all aspects of life.

 **Cultivate a Relationship of Mutual Support:** Supporting and uplifting each other spiritually, emotionally, and physically enhances the marriage bond, fostering a relationship that reflects love and unity.

> The mystery of marriage lies in its unity, where two souls intertwine to create a bond that transcends earthly ties.
> ~ Bertha Bernasko Asante

# CHAPTER 9
# BIBLICAL PRINCIPLES ON SEXUALITY

The Bible holds a rich tapestry of teachings on human sexuality, weaving together themes of love, intimacy, and reverence for the body as a sacred vessel. At the core of these principles is the notion that sexual intimacy is a gift from the divine, to be cherished and expressed within the bounds of marriage. The Scriptures emphasize the importance of mutual respect, honour, and fidelity between partners, calling for a deepening of emotional and spiritual connection alongside physical intimacy. In exploring Biblical narratives, we encounter stories that illustrate the consequences of straying from these principles, highlighting the need for moral discernment and the application of wisdom in navigating the complexities of human desire. Ultimately, the teachings on sexuality found in the Bible offer a roadmap for cultivating a harmonious and fulfilling union that honours both individual dignity and the sacred bond between partners.

> In marriage, unity is a profound mystery, reflecting the divine love that binds us to one another and to the sacred.
> ~ Bertha Bernasko Asante

## Marital Exclusivity:

- **Hebrews 13:4:** "Let marriage be held in honour among all, and let the marriage bed be undefiled, for God will judge the sexually immoral and adulterous."

- The Bible emphasises that sexual activity is meant to be confined to the marital relationship. Anything used within this context would need to align with the understanding that sexual activity should be loving, respectful, and consensual.

## Mutual Respect and Consent:

- **1 Corinthians 7:3-5:** *"The husband should give to his wife her conjugal rights, and likewise the wife to her husband... Do not deprive one another."*

- Sex should be consensual and mutually respectful, ensuring that both partners agree and feel comfortable with the various methods.

## Mutual Respect and Consent:
- **Song of Solomon:** *Celebrating romantic and physical intimacy in marriage, highlighting that love and mutual enjoyment are central to a fulfilling marital relationship.*

- Any method applied should enhance rather than detract from the intimacy and emotional connection between partners.

## Avoiding Temptation and Sin:
- **1 Thessalonians 4:3-5:** *"For this is the will of God, your sanctification: that you abstain from sexual immorality; that each one of you know how to control his own body in holiness and honour."*

- Any practice involving sexual advances should be examined to ensure it does not lead to temptation, objectification, or harm.

## Holistic Consideration:
- **Proverbs 5:18-19:** *"Let your fountain be blessed, and rejoice in the wife of your youth... Let her breasts fill you at all times with delight; be intoxicated always in her love."*

- The Bible encourages a deep and joyous connection in marriage, suggesting that the use of sexual aids should enhance rather than replace the natural and joyful aspects of physical intimacy.

# CHAPTER 10
# CHRISTIAN VIEWS ON SEX

Christian perspectives on sex are shaped by a blend of biblical teachings, traditional doctrines, and the belief that sexuality is a fundamental aspect of God's creation. In the Christian faith, sex is viewed as a gift from God, designed to be expressed within the context of a committed marital relationship. The Bible emphasises the sacredness of sexual intimacy, calling for mutual respect, fidelity, and love between partners. Traditional Christian doctrines often highlight the importance of chastity, self-control, and honouring the body as a temple of the Holy Spirit.

> In marriage, unity is a profound mystery, reflecting the divine love that binds us to one another and to the sacred.
> ~ Bertha Bernasko Asante

Christian teachings also stress the significance of procreation within the marital union, reflecting God's design for the continuation of human life. The notion of sexuality as a sacred and deeply spiritual connection between husband and wife is central to Christian beliefs, emphasising the importance of emotional and spiritual intimacy alongside physical union.

At the core of Christian views on sex is the idea that sexual relationships should be characterised by love, commitment, and mutual consent, with a focus on the well-being and dignity of both partners. These teachings provide a foundation for understanding sex as a beautiful and God-given expression of love and unity within the framework of marriage, highlighting the importance of upholding moral and ethical values in sexual relationships.

## Sex as a Gift from God:

- **Divine Creation:** "Christianity teaches that sex is a gift from God, designed for procreation and the expression of love within marriage. In Genesis 1:28, God blesses the couple and commands them to "be fruitful and multiply."

- **Positive Aspect:** The Bible presents sex as a positive and integral part of human life when expressed within the bounds of marriage.

## Sexual Union Only Within Marriage

- **Exclusive to Marriage:** Christian doctrine emphasises that sexual relations are intended to occur exclusively within the bounds of marriage between one man and one woman. Hebrews 13:4 upholds the sanctity of the marriage bed, stating that marriage should be honoured, and the marriage bed kept pure.

- **Covenantal Relationship:** Sex is viewed as a physical manifestation of the covenantal relationship between husband and wife, symbolising unity and mutual commitment.

## Mutual Love and Respect

- **Intimate Connection:** Ephesians 5:25–28 describes how husbands should love their wives as Christ loves the church, and wives should respect their husbands. This mutual love and respect extend to the sexual relationship, emphasising that both partners' needs and desires should be considered.

- **Selflessness:** Christian teachings encourage selflessness in sexual relationships, focussing on the pleasure and well-being of one's spouse, as seen in 1 Corinthians 7:3-5.

## Purity and Self-Control

- **Avoiding Immorality:** Christians are called to avoid sexual immorality, including premarital sex, adultery, and other forms of sexual behaviour outside of marriage. 1 Thessalonians 4:3-5 encourages believers to live in purity and self-control.

- **Faithfulness:** Faithfulness to one's spouse is paramount, reflecting the commitment and covenant made in marriage. Adultery is condemned in both the Old and New Testaments.

## Holistic Approach to Sexuality

- **Physical and Emotional Aspectsy:** Christianity recognises the importance of both the physical and emotional aspects of sex. It promotes the idea that sexual intimacy should be an expression of love, commitment, and emotional connection.

- **Spiritual Dimension:** Sex is also seen as having a spiritual dimension, reflecting the deep union between Christ and the church (Ephesians 5:31-32).

## Education and Guidance

- **Biblical Guidance:** The Bible provides principles and guidelines for sexual conduct, encouraging couples to seek wisdom and guidance in their sexual relationship.

- **Counselling:** Christian counselling often includes advice on maintaining a healthy and fulfilling sexual relationship, respecting each other's needs, and addressing any issues that arise.

## Restoration and Forgiveness

- **Repentance and Healing:** For those who have struggled with sexual sin or issues, Christianity offers forgiveness and the possibility of restoration. Believers are encouraged to seek God's grace and work towards healing and growth in their relationships.

## Cultural Context

- **Cultural Influence:** While traditional Christian views on sex are rooted in biblical teachings, cultural context and personal interpretation can also influence how these teachings are applied in modern life.

In a nutshell, Christian views on sex are deeply rooted in the belief that sex is a sacred and integral part of the marital relationship. It is celebrated as a gift from God when expressed within the boundaries of marriage, characterised by mutual love, respect, and faithfulness.

# CHAPTER 11
# SEXUAL ENHANCEMENT FOR COUPLES

Absolutely! Enhancing intimacy and connection in a relationship involves a holistic approach that addresses both physical and emotional aspects of the partnership. By combining physical techniques with emotional connection, couples can deepen their bond and create a more fulfilling and satisfying relationship. Prioritizing open communication, exploring new experiences together, building emotional intimacy, and engaging in self-care are just a few ways couples can work towards improving their intimacy, satisfaction, and overall connection. It's important for partners to be attentive to each other's needs, desires, and boundaries in order to foster a deeper level of intimacy and enhance their relationship in a meaningful way.

Here are some varieties of strategies that could be employed to help:

> In marriage, unity is a profound mystery, reflecting the divine love that binds us to one another and to the sacred.
> ~ Bertha Bernasko Asante

## Open Communication

- **Discuss Desires and Boundaries:** Openly talk about your needs, desires, and boundaries with your partner to ensure mutual understanding and respect.

- **Feedback:** Regularly discuss what is working well in your sexual relationship and what could be improved.

## Quality Sleep

- **Prioritise Rest:** Ensure both partners are well-rested, as fatigue can reduce sexual desire and energy levels.

## Physical and Mental Health

 **Healthy Diet:** A balanced diet rich in fruits, vegetables, whole grains, and lean proteins can improve overall health and sexual function.

 **Exercise:** Regular physical activity improves circulation, boosts energy, and enhances mood, all of which can enhance sexual performance.

 **Stress Management:** Use stress-relief techniques like meditation and deep breathing because stress can have a negative impact on libido and sexual performance.

## Mental Connection

- **Emotional intimacy:** Strengthening emotional intimacy through quality time, sharing, and deep conversations can enhance sexual satisfaction.

- **Fantasy Sharing:** Share and explore each other's fantasies in a consensual and respectful way, which can add excitement. Sexual Education

- **Read Together:** Explore books or articles on sexual techniques and intimacy to learn new ways to connect.

- **Attend Workshops:** Couples' workshops on intimacy or sexual health can provide valuable

## Hormonal and Medical Support

- **Consult a doctor:** If there are ongoing issues with sexual function, consult a healthcare provider to explore possible hormonal treatments or other medical solutions.

- **Supplements:** Some couples find benefits from natural supplements like maca root, ginseng, or L-arginine, which are believed to support sexual health (consult with a healthcare provider before use).

### Mindfulness
- **Practice Mindful Sex:** Focus on being fully present during intimate moments, paying attention to the sensations, emotions, and connection with your partner.

### Exploring Different Settings
- **Change of Scenery:** Try making love in various locations or creating a special atmosphere in your usual space with candles, music, or lighting.

- **Role Play:** Consider role-playing scenarios to add an element of fun and creativity to your sexual experiences.

### Intimacy and Foreplay
- **Extend Foreplay:** Spend more time on foreplay to build arousal and enhance the overall sexual experience.

- **Explore New Techniques:** Experiment with distinct types of touch, kissing, and other forms of physical affection to find what feels best for both partners.

### Use of Enhancing Products
- **Lubricants:** Using a good-quality lubricant can reduce friction and increase comfort during sex, especially for women.

- **Massage Oils:** Incorporate massage into your foreplay routine, using scented oils to relax and heighten the senses.

- **Sex Toys:** Some couples introduce sex toys to add variety and excitement to their sexual routine.

- These approaches should be tailored to fit the specific needs and comfort levels of both partners. It is important to remember that sexual enhancement is about mutual satisfaction, respect, and the deepening of the connection between partners.

## Sexual Enhancement Toys: Fantasy or Reality?

There are a number of factors to take into account when discussing the inclusion of toys in a sexual relationship, particularly when considering how personal values, religious beliefs, and mutual respect may influence it.

### Personal Comfort and Preferences:
- **Consideration:** Not all individuals or couples are comfortable with the idea of using toys, and that's perfectly okay.

- **How to approach that:** Respecting each other's comfort levels and preferences is essential. If one partner is uncomfortable, it's important to find other ways to enhance intimacy that align with both partners' needs.

### Communication and consent:
- **Importance:** Open communication and mutual consent are crucial before introducing toys into the relationship.

- **How to tackle that:** Discussing desires, boundaries, and comfort levels ensures that both partners feel respected and comfortable. Consent ensures that both partners are willing participants in any activities involving toys.

### Spiritual and Ethical Considerations:
- **Perspective:** For couples who view their sexual relationship through a religious or spiritual lens, the use of toys may require thoughtful consideration.

- **How to navigate:** Couples should discuss how the use of toys aligns with their values and beliefs, ensuring that it enhances rather than detracts from the intimacy they share.

**Emotional Connection:**
- **Consideration:** It's important to ensure that the use of toys doesn't replace the emotional connection between partners.

- **How to handle that:** Using toys as a supplement rather than a substitute for emotional and physical intimacy may help maintain the relationship's extra connection.

**Mutual Exploration:**
- **Importance:** Toys may be an avenue for mutual exploration, allowing both partners to discover new aspects of their sexual relationship together.

- **How to drive that:** Exploring together may strengthen the bond between partners, fostering trust and deeper intimacy.

**Enhancing Intimacy and Pleasure:**
- **Purpose:** Sex toys may be explored to enhance intimacy and pleasure between partners by introducing variety and new sensations into their sexual experiences.

- **How it is perceived:** Toys may provide stimulation that may not be achievable through manual methods alone, potentially increasing satisfaction for both partners.

**Breaking Monotony:**
- **Purpose:** Some couples employ toys to help break the monotony in long-term relationships by offering new ways to explore each other's bodies and pleasure points.

- **How it is viewed:** Introducing something new may reinvigorate sexual experiences, helping to maintain excitement and connection in the relationship.

**Overcoming Sexual Challenges:**
- **Purpose:** For some couples, toys may assist in overcoming sexual challenges, such as differences in libido, difficulties with arousal, or achieving orgasm.

- **How It Helps:** Toys may provide additional stimulation or facilitate sexual experiences that might otherwise be difficult due to physical or emotional barriers.

Incorporating toys into a sexual relationship can be a positive experience when done with mutual respect, communication, and a focus on enhancing intimacy. However, it's crucial for couples to discuss their feelings, beliefs, and boundaries regarding the use of toys, ensuring that it's a mutually agreed-upon decision and that adds to their relationship rather than complicating it.

## Biblical view on toys?

The Bible does not directly address modern sexual aids or toys, as they were not a concept in biblical times. However, a biblical view on such matters can be inferred from broader principles about sexuality, intimacy, and marital relationships.

From a biblical perspective, the use of sexual toys in marriage is not explicitly condemned or endorsed. The primary concerns are that they should be used in a way that respects the sanctity of the marital relationship, promotes mutual enjoyment and consent, and does not lead to sin or harm.

Couples should consider their personal convictions, communicate openly with each other, and ensure that their practices align with their values and faith.

## Pros and cons of using toys?

Using toys in a sexual relationship can have both advantages and disadvantages. Here's a breakdown of the pros and cons to help you make an informed decision:

Using toys in a sexual relationship may seem to offer benefits, such as enhanced pleasure, variety, and improved communication. However, it's also important to be aware of the potential downsides, such as dependence, reduced emotional intimacy, and discomfort. Open communication, mutual respect, and a focus on maintaining the emotional connection are key to ensuring that the use of toys contributes positively to the relationship.

**Pros of Using Toys:**
1. **Enhanced Pleasure:**
   - **Benefit:** Toys may provide additional stimulation or facilitate sexual experiences that might otherwise be difficult due to physical or emotional barriers.

- **Why It Matters:** This can be particularly beneficial for individuals or couples who may have difficulty reaching orgasm or who want to explore different sensations.

2. **Variety and Exploration:**
    - **Benefit:** Toys introduce variety into the sexual relationship, helping to keep things exciting and fresh. They can be used to explore different fantasies, preferences, and experiences together.
    - **Why It Matters:** Variety can help prevent the relationship from becoming monotonous, maintaining interest and excitement over time.

3. **Assistance with Sexual Challenges:**
    - **Benefit:** Toys can assist in overcoming sexual challenges, such as erectile dysfunction, low libido, or difficulties with arousal. They can also help individuals with physical disabilities or conditions that affect sexual function.
    - **Why It Matters:** This may lead to more fulfilling sexual experiences and help maintain a healthy sexual relationship.

4. **Increased Communication:**
   - **Benefit:** The decision to use toys often requires open and honest communication between partners about desires, boundaries, and comfort levels.

   - **Why It Matters:** This may strengthen the emotional connection between partners and improve overall communication in the relationship.

**Cons of Using Toys**

1. **Potential for Dependence:**
   - **Risk:** Some individuals may become dependent on toys for sexual pleasure, which could lead to difficulties in achieving orgasm or arousal without them.

   - **Why It Matters:** This dependency can create challenges in the sexual relationship, especially if one partner prefers not to use toys.

2. **Variety and Exploration:**
   - **Risk:** Over-reliance on toys could potentially reduce the focus on emotional intimacy, leading to a more mechanical or detached sexual experience.

   - **Why It Matters:** Emotional connection is a vital component of a healthy sexual relationship, and it's important to ensure that toys are used as a supplement, not a substitute, for intimacy.

3. **Discomfort or Disagreement**
   - **Risk:** Not all partners may be comfortable with the idea of using toys. This can lead to discomfort, tension, or disagreement within the relationship.

- **Why It Matters:** It's essential to respect each partner's comfort level and preferences. Forcing or pressuring the use of toys can create resentment or discomfort.

4. **Health and Hygiene Concerns:**
   - **Risk:** If not used or cleaned properly, toys can pose health risks, such as infections or injuries.
   - **Why It Matters:** Proper hygiene, safe use, and choosing high-quality, body-safe toys are essential to prevent any adverse health effects.

5. **Cultural or Religious Conflicts:**
   - **Risk:** The use of toys may conflict with certain cultural or religious beliefs, leading to guilt or internal conflict for some individuals.
   - **Why It Matters:** It's important to consider personal values and beliefs and to discuss these openly with your partner to ensure that both feel comfortable and aligned in their choices.

# CHAPTER 12
# 20 LOVE LANGUAGE FOR COUPLES

**A love language** is an insight that refers to the specific ways in which individuals **express** and **experience** love in a relationship.

The term was popularised by Dr. Gary Chapman in his book *"The Five Love Languages: How to Express Heartfelt Commitment to Your Mate."*

People have different preferences for how they give and receive love, which can be categorised into various basic love languages:

1. **Whispered Affirmations:**
   Sharing loving and affirming words softly in each other's ears, creating a private moment of connection.

2. **Heartfelt Touch:**
   Gently tracing fingers on each other's skin, focusing on areas like the face, neck, or hands to express tenderness without words.

3. **Silent Eye Contact**
   Engaging in extended, meaningful eye contact without speaking, allowing emotions to communicate intimacy.

4. **Secret Gestures**
   Creating a unique gesture or signal that only the two of you understand, used to express love in public or private settings.

5. **Shared Stillness**
   Sitting or lying together in silence, simply enjoying each other's presence without the need for conversation or distraction.

6. **Love messages/letters**
   Writing and exchanging deeply personal letters/ messages, revealing your innermost thoughts and feelings about each other.

7. **Personalised Formalities**
   Creating and maintaining a daily or weekly ritual that is special and meaningful to your relationship.

8. **Slow Dancing**
   Dancing together slowly in a private space, focusing on the connection rather than the rhythm or steps.

9. **Complimentary Breathing**
   Synchronising your breathing while holding each other, creating a sense of unity and calm.

10. **Scent Memory**
    Wearing a particular scent that your partner loves, creating an olfactory connection that triggers fond memories.

11. **Shared Solitude**
    Spending time together in a peaceful setting, like watching the sunset, where you both enjoy the beauty of the moment without distractions.

12. **Intimate Storytelling**
    Sharing personal stories or memories that have shaped who you are, deepening your understanding and connection.

13. **Loving Gaze**
    Giving your partner a soft, loving look from across the room, letting them know they are cherished even in a crowd.

14. **Physical Proximity**
    Sitting or lying closely together, ensuring that you are always touching in some small way, like holding hands or feet intertwined.

### 15. Gentle Kisses

Giving soft, lingering kisses on less common areas like the forehead, palms, or eyelids to express deep affection.

### 16. Morning Connections

Taking a few moments each morning to connect through a brief conversation, cuddle, or touch, setting a positive tone for the day.

### 17. Nighttime Affirmations

Sharing what you love about each other right before falling asleep, reinforcing your bond at the end of the day.

### 18. Intimate Compliments

Complimenting your partner on things that go beyond the physical, like their character, spirit, or the way they make you feel.

### 19. Love Journals

Maintaining a journal together where you both write down thoughts, dreams, and expressions of love, creating a shared narrative.

### 20. Shared Gratitude

Regularly expressing gratitude for each other and the relationship, acknowledging the small and big things that make your connection special.

# CHAPTER 13
# THE BENEFITS OF CORDIAL INTIMACY IN MARRIAGE

Cordial intimacy in marriage refers to maintaining a warm, friendly, and respectful connection between spouses. Cordial intimacy in marriage enriches the relationship by fostering emotional closeness, respect, and mutual support. It creates a positive atmosphere where both spouses feel valued, understood, and loved, which strengthens the marital bond over time.

This type of intimacy can significantly contribute to a marriage's health and strength in many ways:

**Enhanced Communication:** Cordial intimacy fosters open and effective communication between spouses. When there is mutual respect and warmth, couples are more likely to share their thoughts, feelings, and concerns openly and honestly.

**Increased Trust and Understanding:** Being cordial builds trust and understanding within the marriage. When spouses treat each other with kindness and respect, they feel safe to be vulnerable and share their innermost thoughts and emotions.

**Conflict Resolution:** Cordial intimacy provides a foundation for resolving conflicts constructively. Couples who maintain a respectful and friendly demeanour towards each other are better able to navigate disagreements without escalating into hurtful arguments.

**Emotional Support:** Being cordial involves showing empathy and offering emotional support to each other. This creates a supportive environment where spouses feel valued and cared for during both positive times and challenges.

**Physical Affection:** Cordial intimacy often includes expressions of physical affection such as hugs, kisses, and gentle touches. These gestures of warmth and tenderness reinforce the emotional bond between spouses.

**Shared Enjoyment:** Cordial intimacy encourages couples to engage in activities they enjoy together. Whether it is hobbies, outings, or simply spending quality time, sharing enjoyable experiences strengthens their connection.

**Respect for Boundaries:** Being cordial involves respecting each other's boundaries and personal space. This promotes a sense of autonomy and individuality within the marriage while still fostering closeness.

**Long-term Stability:** Couples who maintain cordial intimacy tend to experience greater long-term stability in their relationship. They are more likely to weather challenges and changes together, knowing they have a solid foundation of mutual respect and affection.

**Sense of Partnership:** Cordial intimacy reinforces the idea that marriage is a partnership. Spouses collaborate, support each other's goals and aspirations, and work towards shared dreams and plans.

**Overall Well-being:** Research indicates that strong marital relationships characterised by cordial intimacy contribute to better overall physical and mental health for both partners. They experience lower levels of stress and higher levels of happiness and satisfaction in life.

## FINAL COUNSEL

As you embark on your journey toward deeper intimacy in your marriage, remember that building a strong, lasting connection requires continuous effort, patience, and mutual respect. Intimacy is not just about physical closeness; it is about creating a safe space for emotional vulnerability, intellectual growth, and spiritual unity.

Stay committed to open communication, prioritise your relationship, and lean on the biblical principles that guide you. Let your marriage be a reflection of love, faith, and unwavering commitment. Every small step you take together towards understanding and supporting each other strengthens the foundation of your marriage.

Remember, the journey of cleaving is ongoing—it is about growing together, learning from each other, and continuously nurturing the bond that holds you together. With dedication and love, you can cultivate a marriage that not only endures but flourishes, bringing joy and fulfilment to both of you.

# CONCLUSION

In "Cleaving to Climax: Practical Steps for Deepening Marital Bonds," we have journeyed through the essential elements of intimacy in marriage, exploring how the biblical principle of "leaving and cleaving" forms the foundation for a deeply fulfilling and resilient relationship. The term "cleaving" encapsulates a profound, holistic union that extends beyond mere physical connection, integrating emotional, intellectual, and spiritual dimensions. This commitment to intertwining lives, aspirations, and emotions is pivotal to achieving and sustaining a vibrant marital bond.

From the initial step of leaving behind the old to fully embrace the new partnership to the multifaceted dimensions of intimacy, each chapter of this book has aimed to illuminate the path to a more profound connection between spouses. By emphasising the priority of the marital relationship, fostering various forms of intimacy, and adhering to the teachings of Scripture, couples can build a relationship characterised by unity, mutual support, and enduring commitment. Our exploration of intimacy has highlighted that a fulfilling marriage is built on more than just physical closeness; it involves a deep emotional connection, intellectual engagement, and spiritual unity. The biblical teachings provided in this book serve as a guide to understanding and nurturing these aspects, ensuring that couples can navigate the complexities of life together while maintaining a strong, intimate bond.

As you implement the practical advice and insights offered throughout this book, remember that intimacy is a journey that requires ongoing effort, communication, and mutual respect. By embracing these principles, you will experience the true climax of intimacy—an enriched, joyous relationship that not only withstands the trials of life but also flourishes in love and unity.

# ACKNOWLEDGMENTS

First and foremost, I give all glory to God for the gift of life, for His abundant grace, favour, wisdom, knowledge and empowerment to write this book. Without His divine presence, none of this would have been possible. I am eternally grateful.

To my dear husband, Sam Asante: Your unwavering support, love, care, patience, understanding and encouragement have been my constant source of strength. I salute you. To our exceptionally amazing children, Emmanuel-Cobby, Elvina-Roseline, and Joanita-Eva-Vera: for your love and understanding, and for always inspiring me with your bright spirits. You remind me daily of the beauty of bonding. May your lives be filled with love, joy, peace and tranquillity in your relationships.

I also extend heartfelt gratitude to my mentees and children in Christ—Edna, Evelyn, Anna, Dorcas, Eunice, Grace, Susan, Frederica, Rachel, Esther, and many more including the grandchildren you have brought to my life, they give me so much joy. Your faith and personal growth have been a source of great joy and inspiration for me.

To my dear siblings—Angie, Eva, Jane, Emmanuel, and Alex—thank you for maintaining the deep connection, and strong family bond we were privileged to grow up with in Christ. Your love and diverse support have been invaluable.

I wish to extend my deepest appreciation to my mentors and spiritual parents, under whom I had the honour to serve on the Marriage Committee and as a district leader for the Women's Ministry. Apostle Michael and Mrs. Linda Tedeku, Prophet Emmanuel and Mrs. Joyce Danso, Rev. Delmar and Mrs. Betty Asorwe, Rev. William and Mrs. Josephine Kugbeadjor, and Rev. Ernest and Dr. Mrs Grace Duah—your guidance, hard work, and dedication to building lasting marriages have been instrumental in shaping my journey.

To the ministers in my family who have contributed so richly to my spiritual and personal growth—Bishop and Rev. Mrs. Eva-Vera Hemeng, Rev. Anyimadu, Rev. Solomon and Mrs. Mercy Odame, Rev. Victoria Gyebi, Dcnss Mrs. DSP Agnes Barimah, Dcnss Mrs Gladys Abban, and Pastor Stephen Amoako—I cannot thank you enough for your influence and support.

Furthermore, to my close Christian sisters—Dr. Chim, Deaconesses Monica, Ernestina, Janet, Cecilia, Rita, Sarah, Pat, Dinah, Rose, Lydia, Joyce, Agnes, Florence, Bernice, Linda, Dr Abena, Helen, as well as the entire sisterhood—your love, strength, and spiritual companionship have been a true blessing. I deeply cherish each one of you.

Special thanks to my cherished network communities—CHPNet, NTC Group 73, Wesco Babies, and Taptap Community TV on which I constantly share my expertise. To my women groups, 'Mmaa-Nkomo' Living Spring Women's Ministry, The Eikonic Women, Elegant Eloquent Ladies, and the wonderful PSA Family, especially my ACE Mentors Carole, Netty and Michelle, your able coaching and fellowship gave me the confidence to turn my thoughts and experiences into pages and chapters. I adore you all.

To everyone who has been a part of this journey, thank you from the bottom of my heart. May God continue to bless and guide us all.

# AUTHOR BIOGRAPHY

Bertha Bernasko Asante is a dedicated Christian and a devoted wife with 28 years of marriage. She is a blessed mother with three biological children and countless other adopted children through her extensive mentoring, marital coaching, and counselling. Originally from Ghana and now residing in London, Bertha is a multifaceted professional with roles as a global health educator, marriage counsellor, an author, and public speaker.

With over 28 years of nursing experience, Bertha is currently working as a practice nurse educator and professional nurse advocate. She is deeply committed to championing the well-being of clinical staff and students, providing pastoral support and restorative clinical supervision. Her conflict resolution and problem-solving skills have earned her titles such as "Peacemaker" and "Speaking-Up Advocate."

Academically, Bertha holds a master's degree in healthcare leadership and professional academic practice, along with a Certificate in Christian Counselling. Her academic background complements her practical experience, particularly in marriage and family life, where she has served in various Christian communities, including Scripture Union, PENSA, Girls' Brigade, CHPNet, and the Church of Pentecost UK.

Bertha's passion for marriage and family life is evident in her extensive work, providing premarital counselling, mentoring, and coaching married couples to find fulfilment in their marriages. She started up the "Couples' Reviving Retreat: Join us for a Special Date" a unique program designed to revitalise, rejuvenate, rekindle and strengthen marital bonds.

Her commitment to ministry extends beyond counselling; she actively volunteers with Sunday School and the Youth (Girls Brigade), instilling values of courtesy, integrity, enthusiasm, and aspiration. Her work in various women's, youth, and children's ministries has shaped her as a trusted and influential leader in her community.

In her latest book, Cleaving to Climax: Practical Steps for Deepening Marital Bonds, Bertha draws on her rich experience in marriage, ministry, and counselling to explore the profound dimensions of marital intimacy. She offers practical advice mainly from her encounter with clients, her own numerous years of marriage experience, and grounded in biblical principles. She aims to empower couples to build strong, enduring relationships that flourish in love, unity, and mutual respect.

Concerning book writing, marriage seminars, health education, expert teachings, and keynote addresses, her popular topics include the following:

- Marriage Nuggets: Spice Up Your Union
- Before you take the vows, are you set for companionship?
- Handling Marriage Finance: The Key Principles
- Rebuilding Trust in Relationship: Commit or Resign
- Maintaining intimate pleasure in menopause: Still a necessity
- Sexual dysfunction in marriage: What is the way forward?
- Forgiveness in companionship: Let go and let God heal your marriage.
- Personal hygiene: cleanliness is next to godliness.
- Mind the Messenger: Your Body needs Care

*Cleaving To Climax*

- Complete Body Checkup: Your Guide to Health Assessment

- God's Beautiful Creation, Fearfully and Wonderfully Made

- Back to Reality with Gender: Children Must Know the Basics.

- The Alphabets and Colours: Exploring the Origin of Rainbow

- The Alphabets (LGBTQ) and the Word (BIBLE); in sync or out of sync?

- LGBTQ, who has the right perspective?

- Professional Progression Pathway for Internationally Educated Professionals

Quality Care Compass: Are You All Set for the Care Quality Commissioner Inspection?

*Cleaving To Climax*

Connect with Bertha to stay updated on her latest work and insights on various topics of her expertise:

 **LinkedIn:** Bertha Bernasko Asante

 **Facebook:** Bertha Bernasko Asante

 **Email:** asbeexconsul@gmail.com

 **Website:** asbeexconsul.co.uk

www.ingramcontent.com/pod-product-compliance
Lightning Source LLC
Chambersburg PA
CBHW050434010526
44118CB00013B/1529